|| ॐ **NAMOH BHAGVATE VASUDEVAY NAMAH** ||

GITA GYAN

(SHRIMAD BHAGVADGITA)

IN SIMPLE ENGLISH

BRIJ GUPTA

Pearl Court -2 /803, Essel Towers,
Gurugram, India (Phone 9871664854)

Gita Gyan (Shrimad Bhagvadgita)
Brij Gupta

www.whitefalconpublishing.com

All rights reserved
First Edition, 2021
© Brij Gupta, 2021

No part of this publication may be reproduced, or stored in a retrieval system, or transmitted in any form by means of electronic, mechanical, photocopying or otherwise, without prior written permission from the author.

The contents of this book have been certified and timestamped on the POA Network blockchain as a permanent proof of existence. Scan the QR code or visit the URL given on the back cover to verify the blockchain certification for this book.

The views expressed in this work are solely those of the author and do not reflect the views of the publisher, and the publisher hereby disclaims any responsibility for them.

Requests for permission should be addressed to
brijlalgupta@gmail.com

ISBN - 978-1-63640-216-1

Cover design by White Falcon Publishing, 2021
Cover image source freepik.com
Interior design by Brij Gupta, 2021

PREVIEW

The Bhagavad-Gita is the storehouse of spiritual knowledge in a very concise form. The Lord Krishna Himself, incarnation of God Vishnu, spoke this supreme science of the Absolute Reality which contains essence of all the Vedas and Upanishads and has been presented in a way to be beneficial to the mankind. This knowledge was given in the middle of the battle field to a great warrior Arjun when he was confused and deluded in performing his duties. At the end of the teaching given by the Lord, Arjun confusion got resolved and he became ready for the fight. The teaching and knowledge given in Dvapar Yug is also relevant today for the mankind and will remain so, for all new generations to come. In my personal opinion, one need not study any other scripture if one seriously studies the Gita, contemplates the meaning of the verses, and practices its teachings in one's daily life.

All of us want to be happy and have a peaceful life without any pain and miseries and in this pursuit; we get engaged in endless activities throughout our life but still remain unhappy and disturbed. Sometimes, we do get some happiness but soon we find ourselves lacking in something or the other and again the mind becomes agitated. This cycle goes on in our life. A regular study of the Gita is sure to help you in achieving long lasting peace and happiness. One who is regular in the study of the Gita becomes happy, peaceful, prosperous, and free from the bondage of Karma, though engaged in the performance of worldly duties. It is said that even the sins do not taint those who regularly study the Gita, just as water does not stain a lotus leaf.

The practice of doing selfless service has been beautifully illustrated in the Gita. The sacred knowledge of doing one's duty with the attitude of Karm Yog, whether you get the reward or not, is the core of the teaching, which can lead to Moksh. The Gita is like a ship by which one can easily cross the ocean of this world and become free from the bondage of birth and death. It is also said that wherever the Gita is chanted or read with love and devotion, Lord Makes Himself present there to listen and enjoy the company of His devotees.

There is no need to adopt these so called modern days Gurus to seek worldly happiness as long as one studies Gita daily. However, if you really need a Guru, you need to find someone who himself has studied and understood Gita and also practices the teachings of the Gita. Its teachings are simple as well as difficult to understand and have deep meaning. Every day new and deeper meanings are revealed once you start studying the Gita, and the teachings remain ever inspirational. It is difficult for any ordinary person, or even for the great sages and scholars, to understand the deep, secret meaning of the Gita. To understand the Gita completely is like a fish trying to measure the extent of the ocean, or a bird trying to measure the sky.

I have personally experienced this. I recall in my childhood that my father was so much interested to listen to the Gita every day and since he himself was not able to read and write, he entrusted this responsibility of reading to him one chapter of Gita every day in the morning in Hindi translation published by Gita-Press Gorakhpur. From that day, it has become a habit with me to read one chapter of Gita every day in the morning as my prayer and every time I read the Gita, I find better understanding of the meaning of the verses. It is only after so many years of studying the Gita, reading several books and attending several courses on Gita teachings conducted by Shri Chinmaya Mission and Swami Dayanad Mission, Coimbatore that I got the inspiration to write down the teachings of the Gita in a very simple and easy to understand language. Whatever I have learnt and understood, I have put it in a simple language so that it can also benefit others in the society. If there are any errors or omissions in my writing, I propitiate before Lord Krishna to pardon me and bless me.

JAI SHRI KRISHAN

INDEX

CHAPTER	TITLE	PAGE
	Introduction	1
	What Gita Contains	3
	Summary of Gita Teachings	7
	Description of some important terms used in Gita	26
	Geeta Dhyanam	39
Chapter 1	ARJUN VISHAD YOG	41
Chapter 2	THE KNOWLEDGE OF THE SELF	45
Chapter 3	PATH OF SELFLESS SERVICE	67
Chapter 4	PATH OF RENUNCIATION WITH KNOWLEDGE	83
Chapter 5	PATH OF RENUNCIATION	99
Chapter 6	MEDITATION YOG	111
Chapter 7	GYAN VIGYAN YOG	131
Chapter 8	AKSHAR BRAHM YOG	141
Chapter 9	THE KING OF MOST SECRET KNOWLEDGE	153
Chapter 10	THE GLORIES OF BHAGVAAN	169

CHAPTER	TITLE	PAGE
Chapter 11	COSMIC FORM	179
Chapter 12	THE YOG OF DEVOTION	187
Chapter 13	CREATION AND CREATOR	199
Chapter 14	THE DIVISION OF THREE GUNAS	219
Chapter 15	PURUSHOTAM YOG	231
Chapter 16	DIVINE AND THE DEMONIC QUALITIES	243
Chapter 17	YOG OF THREEFOLD SHRADHA	251
Chapter 18	MOKSH SANYAS YOG	261

INTRODUCTION

Gita is presented as knowledge of the Vedas by Maharishi Vyas in the form of a dialogue between Krishna as Ishvar and Arjun as a human being, an individual. Because the dialogue is between the Lord and a human being, the Gita is called 'Dialogue between God and Man'. Krishna is also presented in Gita as incarnation of God Himself, therefore, Gita can be considered a dialogue between Krishna as avatar of God and a person named Arjun.

Arjun was the greatest archer seated on a chariot and his driver was none other than Lord Krishna. Arjun had ordered his driver to place the chariot in the middle of the two forces of Kauravas and Pandvas so that he could see those in the enemy ranks with whom he has to fight.

Why Shri Krishna had to teach Gita in the middle of the battle field?

Arjun had come to the battle field to perform his duties as a warrior to fight against the forces of his cousin brother Duryodhna who had occupied their kingdom by evil designs. But when he saw his own people, his grandfather Bhishma and his Guru Dronacharya etc. assembled in favour of Duryodhna, he was so much overwhelmed by compassion, sympathy and considerations that he decided not to fight and gave up his bows and arrows. We all know that Arjun had come prepared to the battle field knowing fully well with whom he has to fight against. In fact, he had been waiting for this war for a long time. Until then, there was no problem. Then, why he developed this conflict in his mind in the battle field just before start of the war? He realized the consequences of the war when he was actually faced with the problem of fighting with his own people, his teacher, his elders.

This is what happens with us also in actual life. You understand the implications only when you are faced with a situation. Arjun had affections for his beloved ones and he found himself unable to perform his duties due to his affections. As long as your duty does not come into conflict with your affections, it is easy to perform your duties. However, there are occasions where the affections are more powerful to hinder you from doing your duties as enjoined by Dharma, and this creates conflict within you. This is what happened to Arjun on the battle field when he found himself more moved by affections than by his duty.

This is the unpleasant and embarrassing position of an individual, who is subject to emotions, right and wrong, and also to sorrow. Whenever we are in such conflict, we end up in state of sadness. It was at this time that Arjun asked Krishna to accept him as his disciple and tell him that which is the best for him to do. This is how the teachings of Bhagvad Gita started in the middle of the battle field.

WHAT GITA CONTAINS

Shri Ved Vyas is the author of Bhagavad-Gita. It was he who edited all the four Vedas and made them available to future generations. He presented Bhagavad-Gita in the middle of Mahabharata, which is referred to as fifth Veda. Gita is not as voluminous as Vedas and Upanishads. Gita is referred to as Gita Shastra because it presents the whole matter of Vedas in a very concise form. The title Bhagavad-Gita means the song of the Lord and it is in verse form.

There are 18 chapters and 700 verses in Gita. Each chapter of Gita is named as Yog like first chapter is called Arjun Vishad Yog and so on. Yog is not used here in its usual sense 'to unite' but Yog in the title means the subject matter, first chapter is the subject matter of Arjun's sorrow. Similarly second chapter is titled as Sankhya Yog meaning that Gyan Yog is the subject matter in second chapter, Karm Yog in third chapter and so on.

Out of the total of 700 verses in Gita, first 56 verses (46 verses of chapter 1 and first 10 verses of chapter 2) describe the condition of Arjun's mind when he found himself confused whether he should fight this war or not and surrendered to Lord Krishna and requested His guidance and advise. In addition, there are 7 verses in chapter 11 and 5 verses in Chapter 18, which were spoken by Sanjay to his king Dhritrastra. Therefore, **Bhagvaan gave the entire knowledge called Gita**

Gyan to Arjun in 632 verses in the form of a dialogue between Shri Krishna; the God Himself and Arjun who represents a human being desirous of seeking the knowledge.

WHAT GITA DEALS WITH?

The whole Gita dwells on three words of Vedanta; TAT TVAM ASI. This statement reveals the identity between "You" and the Supreme Lord. The word that reveals the identity between you and the Lord is 'ASI'. The word 'ASI' is to be understood as equal sign in mathematics, so the equation is:

TAT = TVAM

Any mathematical equation does not reveal something that is going to happen later, it is about something which exists now. It does not say; you (TVAM) will become that (TAT). It says *'you are that'*; a very important thing to note. This is whole teaching of Vedanta and Gita is about.

An equation means that two things are equated and necessity for an equation arises when two things seemingly look different from the other. If they are the same but not recognized, only then an equation is written and then we used to prove that equation during our mathematics study. So, an equation means that it is already an existent fact. Jeeva ('you and I') are equated to Brahman; Parmatma; Bhagvaan, by whatever name we may call HIM; i.e. "I AM THAT" and to understand this equation; we have to understand TAT and TVAM. This knowledge about Jeeva and Ishvar has been taught in Gita by Lord Shri Krishna to Arjun in the battle field.

The soul, the Atma in the form of pure consciousness lives in the physical body and this Atma is equated to Paramatma, who **is pure Consciousness and therefore not subject to time, space or attributes. It is pure satya, pure existence and limitless, which is the basis of everything in the universe.** There is nothing that is independent of this satya, 'Param-Brahm' and everything else is nothing but Paramatma. The individual soul is a tiny part of Parmatma, who is infinite bliss. This is called Self-knowledge; the Absolute Truth; the Atma-gyan in Vedanta.

In order to gain this knowledge, it is not necessary to renounce this world and become a Sanyasi but one can gain this Self-knowledge while living in this world and doing daily duties towards family, friends, society and the nation but with the attitude of Karm Yog. All this has been explained in great details in Gita by Lord Krishna to Arjun.

In terms of the teachings given in Gita, every day we have three states:
- wakefulness
- dream, and
- deep sleep,

During a wakeful state, the physical body, mind, intellect, and ego are active.

In a dream state, the individual soul temporarily creates a dream world and wanders in it with a dream body without leaving the physical body.

In deep sleep, the individual soul completely rests in the Eternal Being (the Supreme Soul, Paramatma) without being bothered by mind and intellect.

Supreme Being, the Lord, Ishvar, Paramatma, watches us as a witness during all the three states of wakefulness, dream, and deep sleep.

The individual soul leaves one physical body and takes another body after death. It keeps on acquiring different physical bodies till all Karmas are exhausted; after that, the goal of attaining the Supreme Being is reached. It is a long and difficult spiritual journey to the Supreme abode called Param Dham. And how it can be possible, is described in details in Gita by Lord Krishna.

- **HARI OM -**

SUMMARY OF GITA TEACHINGS

Arjun represents anyone who gets into a conflict and ends up in sadness. Arjun lot is the lot of any human being whose mind is seized with certain situations, which he finds it difficult to handle or gets confused as to what is the right path for him. Arjun recognized this problem in the battle field when he saw all the implications of the war. He realized that he is the loser whether he wins or loses the war. At what cost, he is going to get this kingdom? - by killing such great people as Bhishma and Drona. This kingdom will be of no use without my beloved and respected ones. He starts thinking of in terms of laying down his bow and arrows and lead a life of **Sanyasi**. This is what happens to all of us also when we are faced with such a situation, we get frustrated and become a drop out.

Arjun had been a man of valor, a man of courage, culture and education. So, he offered himself at the mercy of his great friend - Lord Krishna himself and pleaded with Krishna to accept him as his disciple and tell him what the right path is for him. And this is when the teachings began.

In first six chapter of Gita, the meaning of word Tvam, "You" have been unfolded in second chapter starting from 11th verse. The teaching started when Arjun found himself in a dilemma whether to fight or not his own brothers, teachers and relatives etc. and when Arjun surrendered himself to Krishna and sought refuge in Him as a student.

Krishna tells Arjun that there was no reason for sorrow. He begins by saying that you are not this human body but your real nature is Atma, the soul, which is neither the direct doer nor the indirect doer of any action. Therefore, it is free from doer ship as well as enjoyer- ship. Since Atma is not a subject, it cannot be destroyed. Shri Krishna asks Arjun to do his duties knowing this and leaving the results of actions in the hands of the Lord. A wise person, knowing the nature of Atma, becomes free from any limitation, gets liberated and becomes one with the Supreme Being, Parmeshvar.

In 3rd chapter, He then describes two types of life styles – one is called the Karm Sanyas Yog, or the life of renunciation and the other is called the Karm Yog or life of activity. The life style of Karm Sanyas Yog, or the life of a Sanyasi, is not easy one because for that the mind has to be purified and one has to gain control over his sense organs. That means to follow the life of a Sanyasi; certain preparedness is required for the knowledge to become clear to the self. Whereas while remaining in this world, it is easy to follow a life style of relationship, whereby, one can play various roles in the world to get rid of his liking and disliking. Therefore, Krishna asks Arjun to be a Karm Yogi. A Karm Yogi is one who performs all actions without the sense of doer ship, giving up one's **attachment** to the fruits of the actions with full devotion to God.

In the fourth chapter, Shri Krishna first explains that God is unborn and eternal, and He descends on this earth by His Yogic power to establish dharma and protect the saintly people. He then continues to explain Karm Yog again in more details and the Karmic reactions or Laws of Karma. One can attain liberation by performing all actions with the attitude of Karm Yog and in the past also, many ancient sages performed all their works as an act of sacrifice for the pleasure of God and attained liberation.

Then in the fifth chapter Shri Krishna explains that the path of renunciation of actions and the path of doing actions without selfish motive and as a devotion to God, both lead to the same destination of God Realization. However, the renunciation of actions is rather challenging and can only be performed flawlessly by those whose minds are adequately purified first. The Purification of the mind can be achieved only by working in absolute devotion towards God. Therefore, Karm Yog is a more appropriate path for the majority of humankind.

In sixth chapter as well, Shri Krishna continues with the comparative evaluation between Karm Yog; the practice of spirituality while performing worldly duties and Karm Sanyas; the practice of spirituality in renounced state. And then Shri Krishna introduces the topic of Meditation or contemplation upon the Lord; the Ishvar to gain His grace. The sixth chapter therefore is committed to contemplation (meditation), in which Shri Krishna tells how one can fix his mind upon Parmatma by leading the life of a Yogi. This practice of meditation is called Yog because it is meant for uniting the mind with God.

From the seventh chapter onwards, there is a complete change in the presentation of the subject matter to the word TAT, "that", meaning the Lord, Parmeshvar who is the cause of everything, and remains the central topic in next six chapters.

In the seventh chapter, two types of Prakriti of the Lord were mentioned briefly. One Prakriti consisting of three qualities and divided into eight factors is called Apara Prakriti because it is the cause of the sansaar. The other Para Prakriti is the essential nature of the Lord. Because of these two Prakriti, the Lord, gains the status of Creator, Sustainer and Destroyer of the world. Both Atma and Maya are also called Prakriti because both are the cause of the creation.

In eighth chapter, Shri Krishna explains that in order to attain God, Brahman, one must remember God at the time of death. The cycle of creation and dissolution is also explained as how the creation manifests from Brahma and how at the time of dissolution, everything dissolves back into Him. However, the divine Abode of God is untouched by this cycle of creation and dissolution.

In ninth chapter, Shri Krishna reveals the science of loving devotion to God. He explains that there is only one God, who is the sole object of worship. For all living beings, He is the true friend, the support, refuge, and the final goal. Therefore, those souls who engage in exclusive devotion towards the Supreme Lord go to His abode and remain there. However, those who perform Vedic rituals for certain materialistic gains, go to the celestial abodes after death and return to earth when the merits of their good deeds are exhausted.

In tenth chapter, Shri Krishna describes His infinite glories and opulence and reveals that He is the source of all that exists; everything that exists is a manifestation of His energies. Whatever catches our imagination and infuses us with bliss is nothing but a tiny spark of His opulence. Then in Eleventh chapter Shri Krishna reveals His infinite cosmic Form or vishwswarup. And then in Twelfth chapter, Shri Krishna describes the path of Bhakti, the path of true devotion towards His personal Form which is easier to practice for human beings.

The last six chapters deal with the identity between the two - identity between *individual soul or Jeevatma* and the Supreme Lord; the Paramatma. Shri Krishna explains that in reality, **the individual Atma is same as Paramatma himself**. To know this and realize this, the real knowledge is to be gained. Sri Krishna says this knowledge is very secret and difficult to understand by a common man. Only by following the life of Karm Yogi, one can prepare his mind to gain this knowledge and attain Moksh, liberation from the cycle of birth and death.

This world has been called mṛiga tṛiṣhṇā in the scriptures, meaning "like the mirage seen by the deer." The sun rays reflecting on the hot desert sand create an illusion of water for the deer. It thinks there is water ahead of it and runs to quench its thirst. But the more it runs toward the water, the more the mirage fades away. Its dull intellect cannot recognize that it is running after an illusion. The unfortunate deer keeps chasing the illusory water and dies of exhaustion on the desert sand. Similarly, the material energy Maya too creates an illusion of happiness, and we run after that illusory happiness in the hope of quenching the thirst of our senses. But no matter how much we try, happiness keeps fading further away from us.
Kathoupnishad states; "When one eliminates all selfish desires from the heart, then the materially fettered Jeevatma (soul) attains freedom from birth and death, and becomes Godlike in virtue."

CONCLUSION OF FIRST 12 CHAPTERS

People are born different. A single method or system cannot meet the spiritual needs of all. Therefore, Lord Krishna tells about four paths that can lead to God.

1. The Path of devotional worship, offering prayers to the Lord, practicing a life of spiritual discipline such as a ritual, or worship of Lord various Forms like Vishnu, Mahesh, Krishna, and Rama that suits an individual. This path is easy to follow for emotional people.
2. Path of meditation for contemplative people - focus your mind on Ishvar, Paramatma and let your intellect dwell upon the Lord alone through meditation and contemplation. Shri Krishna says this path of meditation is better than the path of devotional worship.
3. Path of Sanyas or Path of Gyan Yog - Whereby one renounces all worldly activities and dedicates all actions to the Lord just as an instrument to serve and please Parmatma and spends all his life in pursuit of self-knowledge. Shri Krishna says though this path is better than the previous two paths but it is difficult to practice unless the mind is fully prepared for it.
4. Path of Karma Yoga – just surrender unto the Lord's will and renounce the attachment to, and the anxiety for, the fruits of all actions by learning to accept all results. This is the selfless service to humanity for householders. This is the path which

needs to be followed by every human being while living in this world and doing one's duties towards the family, towards the society and the nation with the attitude of Karm Yog. By following this path, one's mind gets purified and gets prepared to gain the Knowledge of the Self and gain Moksh.

CONCLUSION OF LAST SIX CHAPTERS

God can be realized in varying degrees of closeness. Let us understand this through an example. Suppose you are standing by the railway tracks. A train is coming from the distance, with its headlight shining. It seems to you as if a light is approaching. When the train comes closer, you can see a shimmering form along with the light. Finally, when it comes and stands on the platform in front, you realize, it's a train and you can see all these people sitting inside their compartments, and peeping out of their windows. The same train seemed like a light from far. As it came closer, it appeared to have a shimmering form along with the light. When it drew even nearer, you realized that it was a train. The train was the same, but on being closer to it, your understanding of its different attributes such as shape, colour, passengers, compartments, doors, and windows grew.

Similarly, God is perfect and complete, and is the possessor of unlimited energies. His personality is replete with divine Names, Forms, Pastimes, Virtues, Associates, and Abodes. However, He is realized in varying levels of closeness, as the Brahman (formless all-pervading manifestation of God), the Paramatma (the

Supreme Soul seated in the heart of all living beings, distinct from the individual soul), and Bhagvaan (the personal manifestation of God that descends upon the earth). The Bhagavatam states:

"There is only one Supreme Entity that manifests in three ways in the world—Brahman, Paramatma, and Bhagvaan." They are not three different Gods; rather, they are three manifestations of the one Almighty God. However, their qualities are different. This is just as water, steam, and ice are all made from the same substance—H_2O molecules; but their physical qualities are different. If a thirsty person asks for water, and we give ice, it will not quench the thirst. Ice and water are both the same substance but their physical properties are different. Similarly, Brahman, Paramatma, and Bhagvaan are manifestations of the one Supreme Lord but their qualities are different.

Brahman is the all-pervading form of God, which is everywhere.

The Śhwetāśhvatar Upanishad states:

"There is only one Supreme Entity. He is seated in everything and everyone." This all-pervading aspect of the Lord is called Brahman. It is full of eternality, knowledge, and bliss. However in this aspect, God does not manifest His infinite qualities, enchanting personal beauty, and sweet Pastimes. He is like a divine light that is nirguṇa (without qualities), nirvivśeṣh (without attributes), nirākār (without form).

Those who follow the path of Gyan-Yog worship this aspect of God. This is a distant realization of God as a formless light, just as the train from far appeared like light.

Paramatma is the aspect of God that is seated in everyone's hearts. In verse 18.61, Shree Krishna states: "O Arjun, the Supreme Lord dwells in the hearts of all living beings. According to their karmas, He directs the wanderings of the souls, who are seated on a machine made of the material energy." Residing within, God notes all our thoughts and actions, keeps an account of them, and gives the results at the appropriate time. We may forget what we have done, but God does not. He remembers our every thought, word, and deed, since we were born. And not only in this life; but in endless lifetimes, wherever we went, God went along with us. He is such a friend who never leaves us for even a moment. This aspect of God dwelling within is the Paramatma. Just as the train, which appeared as light from far, was seen as a shimmering form when it came closer, similarly, the realization of the Supreme Entity as Paramatma is a closer realization than Brahman.

Bhagvaan is the aspect of God that manifests with a personal form.

The Shreemad Bhagavatam states:

"The Supreme Lord Who is the Soul of all souls, has descended upon the earth in His personal form, as Shri Krishna, for the welfare of the world." In this Bhagvaan aspect, God manifests all the sweetness of His Names, Forms, Qualities, Abodes, Pastimes, and Associates. These attributes exist in Brahman and Paramatma as well, but they remain latent, just as fire is latent in a match-stick, and only manifests when it is struck against the igniting strip of the matchbox. Similarly, as Bhagvaan, all the powers and aspects of God's personality, which are latent in the other forms, get revealed.

The path of Bhakti, or devotion, leads to the realization of the Supreme Entity in His Bhagvaan aspect. This is the closest realization of God, just as the details of a train become visible when it comes and stops in front of the observer. Hence, in verse 18.55, Shri Krishna states: "Only by loving devotion can I, the Supreme Divine Personality, be known as I am." Thus, Shri Krishna emphasizes that He considers the devotee of His personal form to be the highest yogi.

HUMAN VALUES IN GITA

The Gita tells us how to manage our life by acquiring the different values. The aim of value education is to prepare good people, necessarily not religious people. The Bhagavad Gita may be referred for different human values for peaceful and joyful living at any time under any circumstances. They are helpful for Self-Realization and Liberation. These values are mentioned in different chapters of Gita.

First value is in chapter 2 – be a Sthit pragya – a person with steady mind and intellect.

A person or a noble person with steady mind is one:
- Who is free from all desires as and when they appear in his mind and remains happy with himself and within himself.
- Who is not attached to anything meaning that, he does not rejoice on getting the desired results and does not get perturbed by the undesired situation.
- Who has evenness of mind meaning that he remains same in pleasure and pain, victory and defeat, heat and cold.
- Who does his duties in a selfless manner as a Karm Yogi and remains unattached to fruits of actions. He has no longings for worldly objects and thus remains free from fear and anger. He acts not for his crave for fruits of actions but for the sake of his duties only in the spirit of Karm yoga. He is free from passion, fear and anger.

Second Value is in Chapter 4 – to lead a life of Disciplined Actions

- A person should do his duties without any selfish attachment to the fruits of actions. He is free from all expectations and accepts the results of actions happily without any grudge whether it is below his expectations or even opposite to his expectations.
- A person should perform all actions as a service to the almighty, remaining always contented and not depending upon anything.
- A person should remain fully engaged in the activities of life, to sustain his body, thinking that

he is not the doer of these actions. He is content with whatever comes to him naturally.
- While doing his duties, he remains unaffected by pairs of opposites such as likes and dislikes, success and failure.
- One should perform all actions as a service to the almighty, every action for him is a holy sacrifice, a holy act and he perceives Lord in every action.

Third Value in Chapter 12 is - Devotion (Bhakti)

A person, who lives a life of Devotee of the God, has following values in him:
- He has supreme faith in God
- He has control over his sense organs and sense objects
- He is free from ego
- He is compassionate, contemplative, totally dedicated to God with firm conviction with mind and intellect.
- He does not envy any one, is friendly, forgiving, always contended, joyful and without any hatred for any one.

Fourth Value in chapter 13 is to inculcate certain qualities that help to acquire self Knowledge

A true understanding of the creator and his creation is true knowledge. A person, who has true knowledge of Paramatma, has following values:

1. Absence of ego, meaning refraining from self praise and not to demand respect from others for the knowledge he has.
2. Not to demand respect without having any qualification for it.
3. Not hurting living beings including plants and trees.
4. Having composed mind that does not react orally or physically when he is harmed or abused in any way by someone.
5. Straight person having alignment between thoughts, word and deeds.
6. Having respect and love for the teacher or Guru and remaining connected with the Guru to have the knowledge with great devotion and faith in him.
7. Cleanliness or purity internally and externally.
8. Steadfastness, remaining steady in your commitment to your duties or in your pursuit to gain liberation.
9. Having control over your body, mind and senses meaning to withdraw your sense organs from worldly pleasures.
10. Having natural dispassion towards sense pursuits, giving up longings.

11. Absence of pride, absence of "I". "me" and "mine" notions.
12. Remaining unaffected and unperturbed, not getting upset or unhappy in birth, death, old age, disease etc.
13. Absence of ownership, or not getting attached to his possessions.
14. Absence of excessive affection towards anything.
15. Evenness of mind in gain or loss of desirable and undesirables. One should accept the results of actions as it comes, as a Prasad of Ishvar.

Fifth Value in Chapter 14 is to be a 'Gunateet', to be free from all three Gunas

A Gunateet is one who has arisen above all the three qualities of Satv, Rajas and Tamas, meaning that he has come out of the attractive power of Maya and Prakriti. He remains unaffected whether he is under the spell of Satvic qualities, Rajsic qualities or Tamsic qualities. He knows that whatever is happening is the role of three qualities of the Prakriti and Bhagvaan Maya and therefore does not get affected by any of these qualities.

Sixth Value in Chapter 16 is to have Divine Qualities

There are 26 Divine tendencies of a person of Daivi Prakriti, which are described in chapter 16 in details. Some of these are also part of the fourth value described above.

QUESTIONS ASKED BY ARJUN IN GITA

In Bhagwad Gita, Arjun asked sixteen sets of questions from Shri Krishna, which are:

1. Who is sthit pragya – the wise person situated in divine consciousness; how he talks, how he sits and how does he walks. (Verse 2.54)

2. If you consider knowledge is better than actions, then why do you want me to do actions and indulge in this horrible war? Please tell me clearly the one path by which one can attain highest good. (Verse 3.1)

3. Why a person commits sinful acts, unwillingly and unknowingly as though driven by force?" (Verse 3.36)

4. How can I understand that you gave this knowledge in the beginning of the creation while your birth is recent?" (Verse 4.4)

5. You praised the path of renunciation of actions, and again you praised path of doing work with devotion and

renouncing attachment to results. Please tell me decisively which of the two is more beneficial?" (Verse 5.1)

6. The mind is very restless, turbulent, strong and obstinate. It appears to me that it is more difficult to control than the wind. (Verse 6.33, 34)

7. What is the fate of a yogi who has full devotion, but whose mind deviated from the spiritual path since he could not keep his mind under control and thus was unable to yogic perfection in this life? (Verse 6.37, 6.38, 6.39)

8. What is Brahman, Adhyatam and Karma. What is Adhibhūta, and who is said to be the Ādhidaiva. Who is Ādhiyagya and how he Adhiyagya. And how one with steadfast mind can remember you at the time of death? (Verse 8.1 & 8.2)

9. After praising Lord Krishna as the supreme divine personality, the Eternal God, the creator and Lord of all beings, and the Lord of the Universe, Arjun requests Lord Krishna to describe the divine opulence, the divine glories by which you pervade all the worlds. (Verse 10.12 to 10.18)

10. After listening to the most secret spiritual knowledge from Shri Krishna and His divine glories, Arjun now wanted to see the divine cosmic form of the Supreme Lord. (Verse 11.1 to 11.4)

11. After witnessing the almost unbelievable cosmic form of Lord Krishna, Arjun had realized that Shri Krishna is the Supreme Lord who existed before all creation and He is the God of all gods. Having become bewildered and agitated, he wanted to know the true nature of the Supreme Lord and His purpose of taking avatar in this human form. (Verse 11.31)

12. Arjun wanted to know which devotee is better of the two - those who worship the human form of God with full devotion in Him or those who worship the formless Absolute Supreme Reality. (Verse 12.1)

13. In most editions of Bhagavad-Gita, this question of Arjun has been omitted (verse 13.1) and Shri Krishna answers this question by himself anticipating that Arjun would ask this. The question which Arjun wanted to ask was – what is Prakriti (Nature) and Puruś (the enjoyer), kṣhetra and kṣhetragya; Gyan (true knowledge) and gyey (object of knowledge)

14. Who is a Gunateet (who have risen above the three guṇas), how do they conduct and how does one transcend the three gunas. (Verse 14.21)

15. What happens to a person who worship God with full faith and devotion but unknowingly disregard the injunctions given in the scriptures. **(Verse 17.1)**

16. Arjun wanted to know the distinction between sanyās (renunciation of actions) and tyāg (renunciation of the desire for the fruits of actions); (verse 18.1)

In addition to above 16 set of questions, Arjun described the Cosmic Form of Lord Krishna in 16 verses from 11.15 to 11.30 and then praises the glories of Lord Krishna and finally requesting Him to resume His human Form, in subsequent 11 verses 36 to 46 of Chapter eleven.

- HARI OM -

DESCRIPTION OF SOME IMPORTANT TERMS USED IN GITA TEACHING

Definition of 'Action'; KARM

Action takes place based on desire and will as well as types of thoughts in the mind. The action can be done by three means - The physical body, Organ of speech and the mind. Physical body here refers to hands, legs that are used to perform the work. Any action that is done can be grouped under any of these three means of actions – for example, when you offer a prayer, it can be verbal or mental action or a ritual involving physical limbs. However, all the three involve the mind. No action is possible without the involvement of mind or intellect.

Also, for every action to take place, there are number of other factors because of which action is made possible, these are called karak in Sanskrit. There are six factors:

- Doer or karta, or agent of action is first karak.
- Object of action – what has to be achieved or gained
- The Instrumental means by which the action is done is third karak
- The purpose of one's actions is the fourth karak, the purpose may be to fulfil one's desire for wealth or to do selfless service to someone etc.
- Fifth karak is the status or position from where the action has to be undertaken, meaning if the action

has to be done from very beginning or from midway.
- The sixth factor is the status of the object of the action for example where does the object exists; is it seen or unseen or has it been achieved before or not etc.

Based on these factors, the action is undertaken by any or all of the three means described above. The action itself is of two types:

1. Action which is to be done is called enjoined action, or action according to Dharma for example helping another person is Vihit **Karm**.
2. Actions which are not to be done are called prohibited actions **(Nishidh Karm)** like killing any living being is a prohibited action.

What is inaction (Akarm)?

Generally it is understood that absence of action is inaction. When a man who is walking, stops walking, action of walking has stopped, he is standstill, and no action is done in terms of physics since there is no motion involved. But standstill is still an action, because it also involves energy to stand, similarly sitting also involves action, which is why you cannot do it for long.

However, in Vedic philosophy, Akarm is the Karm that is done without selfish motive and without attachment to the fruits of actions. These actions do not bind the person to the world but liberate one from the cycle of birth and death. Therefore, inaction is those actions which are devoid of pride and done with the attitude of surrendering the results of actions to God. For example, if we do any ritual without any desire to get something in return for ourselves or we work for welfare of the mankind like providing food to the hungry without any selfish motive, then these actions are considered to be inaction, or virtuous act which helps in liberation.

THE MEANING OF SHREYAS AS DESCRIBED IN GITA ?

Usually, what is good for you at a given time is not good for you at another time. For example - a particular drug may cure your illness but once it is cured, it is not good for you and may do some harm if you continue taking it. Similarly, one drug that treats your problem may not be good for someone else with the same problem, because that person may be allergic to the drug. This kind of goodness is called relative goodness, something that is not always applicable in the same way. Relative goodness is determined by place, time and situation and it keeps changing.

Absolute goodness is one that does not change at any time and is always the same for any person, in Sanskrit, absolute goodness is called Shreyas.
Shreyas, in Gita, is defined as complete acceptance of oneself. You should be acceptable to yourself without any

condition or attributes, without even the physical body and its condition. If the body is something on the basis of which you have self-acceptance, you are in trouble because the body will keep changing with time. The body is time bound. The Self by itself, in its own glory, should be acceptable to you.

ATTACHMENT AS EXPLAINED IN GITA

We do not own any thing in this world. Everything has been given to us and because it has been given to us, it can be taken away at any time. We only happen to possess a few things in our life from time to time. Some of these possessions like son, wife, parents or other siblings with whom we have interactions for a long time may also last for a long time. We develop so much identity with them that when they are doing well, we are happy, when they are not, we become miserable. If any of these possessions are lost, one feels as if he is also lost. This all happens due to our **excessive attachments** to our possessions. It is not simply affection but there is too much emotional dependence.

We all know virtue of patience but most of us are impatient and sometimes become nervous and abusive over small things in our day to day life costing us peace of mind. Though we all know that we have little control over most of the problems but we tend to believe that we are the driver of the events in our life.

There is nothing wrong in having care and affection. These are healthy positive expressions that help a person to grow spiritually. **The problem is not affection or attachment but emotional dependence, called excessive attachment, which makes us sad and unhappy.**

There are other possessions, for which we may not have affection, but we might get attached to them like our house, car, furniture, gold jewelry etc. and take good care of them. Caring to certain extent for these worldly objects or your children, siblings etc. is alright and there is nothing wrong in that. However, when there is excessive caring to the point of causing you anxiety, tension and any kind of pain, it turns into **attachment and not caring.** Love and care to certain extent are fine but not more than that. When it becomes emotional dependence, it creates a problem for you and others. The one, who is loved, becomes a source of pain and sorrow for you.

However, there is a very fine line between attachment and caring which is not easy to discern. Then how do we overcome our excessive attachment or emotional dependence on them? Freedom from attachment means that our attitude and/or reaction should remain same when the person whom we love and care for, does not behave according to our expectations or even under the circumstances if we lose them.

We all must have experienced that when situation is desirable, our mind is cheerful and if not, it is sorrowful.

Things keep changing and if the mind also changes along with them, becoming elated with the desirables and depressed with the undesirables, our life becomes miserable. One needs to keep trying to maintain composure under all situations, whether it is desirable or undesirable. If one knows swimming, he is not bothered about depth of water, similarly when one has composure of mind; it does not matter whether the situation is desirable or undesirable. This is not easy to attain, but by practice one needs to reduce emotional dependence in order to remain happy in life.

What is Puny and Paap?

Puny is a Sanskrit word that means virtuous', 'righteous and sacred act. Puny is referred to as good karma or a virtue that contributes benefits in this and the next birth and can be accumulated by appropriate means according to the law of the universe and human behavior. In Vedanta, Punya is the invisible wealth, or unseen fruits of actions that result into happier rebirth on earth or a long sojourn in heaven. Helping others in need, courage to speak the truth, practicing honesty, being kind and courteous towards all living beings and lead a spiritual life are all some of the examples of Punya Karm.

On the other hand, **Paap** is referred to as bad karmas or any action by physical body, word or thought which harm or can harm the doer or the fellow humans or any fellow beings on the earth or anywhere in the cosmos, immediately or at a later period of time. In Vedanta, all such actions are termed as sin which are also unseen fruits of actions that result that into pain and sorrow to doer in this life and rebirth in lower species of life. These are the karmic debts which bind the person to the cycle of death and birth.

Any action when it is done solely for fulfilling desires or likes and dislikes by unlawful or wrong means result into paap according to Vedanta and are also called dushkarm.

Moksh, the ultimate goal of life?

Moksh literally means liberation or freedom from something which you do not want. It also means release from bondage. What is this bondage from which we want to be liberated? It is the bondage of the body, bondage with our desires and Karmas done to fulfill those desires. Once we get released from these bondages, we accomplish Moksh and get freed from the cycle of birth and death, from the 'sansaar' which is full of pain and sorrows.

In Vedanta, the soul of an individual human being is referred to as Atma while the soul of the Supreme Being is referred to as Paramatma. It is when a human soul realizes that it is just a part of the supreme soul. The individual Atma merges into Paramatma and that Atma is said to have attained Moksh.

Everyone wants to be free from insecurity, free from any pain and wants to be happy always. In life, we gain so many things and anything which is gained, will certainly be lost in time, even the body will get lost at some time; so nothing will stay permanently with us. Even death is not an end in itself since after death, we are reborn and life begins again. However, when we accomplish Moksh, there is no return since Moksh is the end because it is not what is gained or reached, but it is an accomplished fact by gaining self-knowledge, knowledge of Atma. And once the true nature of Atma is well understood, one gets liberated since Atma is always liberated. *Moksh is not after death, but while living.*
Moksh is not an equivalent to salvation, nor is it some kind of accomplishment. Moksh is also not freedom from wealth and desires and Dharma. Moksh is freedom from being insecure and unhappy and this freedom can be attained only by the Divine knowledge or God Realization and as soon as you realise this, you get released from the bondage of birth and death.

Kama, Raag and Dvesh as in Gita

The word Kama in Sanskrit has two meanings – the desire itself and the objects of desire. The thought process wherein you want to gain an object is called a desire and that which you desire is also called a desire.

In common Indian concepts, Kama denotes longing and desire, often with a sexual connotation. But the broader concept refers to any wish, passion and pleasure of the senses, affection, love or enjoyment of life. In the Upanishads and in Gita, the term Kama is used in the broader sense of any type of desire and longing.

Desire or Lust is a longing for objects which are not with you, which are away from you and you want to accomplish that, you want to possess that. If you are unable to accomplish that, it brings you sorrow, unhappiness and sadness and eventually results into anger.

The objects of desire can be seen or unseen – seen are those which you get now and unseen something which you get later. Suppose a man performs a ritual, havan etc for the purpose of gaining something here in this world. By performing that ritual, he gains a certain grace of God or gains Puny which removes all obstacles to his efforts to gain what he wants. He may or may not get, that is altogether different since it will all depend upon if he has done that ritual with total faith and as per shastras or not.

Raag and Dvesh are generally used together. The word Raga in Sanskrit means attachments to the objects which we already have and do not want to part away with. If you lose them, it is cause of sorrow to you and ultimately which again causes anger in you. The word Dvesh in Sanskrit means aversion or dislike for objects which you do not want to possess or you want to be away from. The dislike is so much that it turns into hatred and if by any chance, you get that object, it also brings sorrow and anger in you.

In Gita, it is emphasized that Kama, Raag and Dvesh should be acknowledged and fulfilled in a balanced way so that the sadhak can move toward freedom from desire, rather than getting caught up in the cycle of increasing desire, overindulgence and greed.

WHO IS GURU?

In Vedanta, Guru is one who is a teacher to impart spiritual knowledge. There are two letters in the word GURU – GU meaning darkness or ignorance and RU meaning the one who removes it. Thus a Guru is one who removes darkness of ignorance by teaching the Shastras and who is able to unfold the meaning of the words contained in Shastras.

Our own Soul inside us is the divine Guru. Outside teachers only help us in the beginning of the spiritual journey. Our own mind — when purified by selfless service, prayer, meditation, worship, silent chanting of Lord's name, congregational chanting of holy names, and scriptural study becomes the best channel and guide for the flow of divine knowledge. The Divine Being within all of us is the real Guru, and one must learn how to tune in with Him. It is said that there is no greater Guru than one's own mind. A pure mind becomes a spiritual guide and the inner divine guru leading to a real guru and Self-realization. This is expressed by the common saying that the guru comes to a person when he or she is ready. The word "guru" also means vast and is used to describe the Supreme Being, the divine guru and internal guide.

The wise spiritual teacher disapproves of the idea of blind personal service, or the guru cult, which is so common in India. A Self-realized master says that God only is the guru, and all are his disciples. A disciple should be like a bee seeking honey from flowers. If the bee does not get honey from one flower, it immediately goes to another flower and stays at that flower as long as it gets the nectar. Idolization and blind worship of a human guru may become a stumbling block in spiritual progress and is harmful to both the disciple and the guru.

WHAT IS HAPPINESS?

Happiness is of two types – Absolute happiness which is internal happiness and long lasting. This Absolute Happiness does not depend upon any gain, any accomplishment or anything. It is not born out of any piece of knowledge, or gain of any object. It is just the recognition of yourself, recognized by the intellect and beyond sense perceptions.

Second is Relative Happiness which is based on gaining some sense objects. The relative happiness can thus be one of the following....

- Vidya Sukha, the happiness which you get by gaining the knowledge. But it is also a temporary happiness, once the challenge is over, or exam is over and you pass the examination and go to next higher class, the happiness which you got by

passing the previous exam is gone. Thus Vidya Sukha includes any accomplishment.
- Vishya Sukha – the happiness which you get when your desire for a particular object gets fulfilled. This is also temporary happiness since once one desire gets fulfilled, new desires takes birth in the mind and you start craving to achieve that and make you miserable till you achieve that and so on.

Happiness born of Yog (meaning prayer, meditation); you get happiness from doing prayers and meditation and it is experienced by a disciplined person. Mastery over the mind means one is not carried away by its various moods; it has to remain in state of great composure in all situations. This happiness achieved by remaining in Yog is absolute happiness.

WHAT IS YOG?

The word Yog is derived from root 'YUJ', which has two meanings – 'Yog' and 'Nirodh'. Yog means connecting or uniting two things, so when two things are put together, it is Yog. Nirodh means control, stopping, mastering meaning Yog is the mastery of one's thinking process, and Yog is discipline by itself.

In Gita, Yog is used in both context – Union and control. It has to be seen in what context it has been used in which verse. Just by sitting in *Yoga* posture and trying to do meditation when we have so much attachment to sense objects, we cannot attain the status of being a *Yogi*. Also, as you know Krishna gave this knowledge of *Yog* in the battle field and called him to get up and fight. He never asked Arjun to give up this world, renounce your right to the throne, give up all work and practice this *Yog*. The beauty of Gita teaching is to attain that status while living in this world, performing all your responsibilities as a father, as a son, brother, friend etc.

A Yogi has been used in three ways in Gita in different chapters –

1) Karm Yogi - who is committed to life of actions in selfless way without getting attached to the results of the actions surrendering the fruits of action to the God,

2) Dhyan Yogi - who is committed to life of meditation on Parmatma, Brahman.

3) Gyan Yogi - who is committed to life of gaining the true knowledge of the Atma and Parmatma.

A yogi is called an accomplished person whose contemplation has been successful that he has no longing for any object, known or unknown, visible and invisible.

- HARI OM -

GEETADHYANAM

I invoke you 'O' Bhagavad-Gita, the mother of Goddess, taught by Bhagvaan Narayan himself for Arjun, faithfully collected and reported by ancient sage Vyas and placed in the middle of Mahabharata, in 18 chapters showering the nectar of nonduality and destroying the life of repeated births.

My salutations to Vyas first who lit this lamp of knowledge well by filling it with the oil of Mahabharata. My salutations to Lord Krishna, who is the symbol of knowledge and who as a boatman, helped Pandvas cross the river of battle.

The Upanishads are the cow, Krishna is the milker, Arjun is the calf, the one whose mind is clear is the drinker of this milk and invaluable timeless Gita is the milk coming out from Upanishads.

I salute Lord Krishna, the teacher of the world, the Lord of Lakshmi, wealth, whose nature is fullness, whose grace makes a mute person to speak eloquently and a lame person to climb mountains.

My salutations to the Lord about whom all gods from Brahma ji onwards, sing hymns of praise. To whom, various scholars and contemplative people also pray. And whose glories are not known to even gods and demons.

OM SHANTI SHANTI

The Supreme Lord; Bhagvaan

The Supreme Lord; Bhagvaan dwells in all physical bodies in this universe.

HE is complete, ultimate seer, the great guide and the sustainer, destroyer and creator of the whole cosmos.

I invoke HIS grace to bestow upon me to be able to write this book on SHRIMAD BHAGVADGITA GYAN.

CHAPTER 1 – Arjun Vishad Yog

The war of Mahabharata has begun after all negotiations by Lord Krishna and others to avoid it had failed. The blind King (Dhritarashtra) was never very sure about the victory of his sons (Kauravas) in spite of their superior army. Sage Vyas, the author of Mahabharata, wanted to give the blind king the boon of divine eyesight so that the king could see the horrors of the war for which he was primarily responsible. But the king refused the offer. He did not want to see the horrors of the war; but preferred to get the war report through his charioteer, Sanjay. Sage Vyas granted the power of clairvoyance (**Divya Dhrishti**) to Sanjay. With this power, Sanjay could see, hear and recall the events of the past, present, and the future. He was able to give an instant replay of the eye-witness of the war report to the blind King sitting in the palace. Sanjay is thus narrating to Dhritrashtra what he saw in the battle field on the first day just before the start.

Both the armies of Kauravas and Pandvas are standing in the battle field ready for the war. Duryodhna is describing to Guru Dronacharya about all the warriors of his army as well as that of Pandvas. Kaurvas army is led by Bhishma Pitamah while the army of Pandvas is led by Dhrishtdhuman, the son of King Drupad. Kauravas army blew their conches, cymbals, drums, trumpets etc. to declare the start of the war from their side. After that, Lord Krishna, seated in a grand chariot yoked with white horses, blew his celestial conch followed by Arjun and all other commanders of various divisions of the army of

Pandvas. Hearing the tumultuous uproar, resounding through the earth and sky, Dhritrastra's sons were trembling in fear.

After that, when the war was just to begin, Arjun lifting his bow, asked Shri Krishna to place his chariot between the two armies so that he could see those people who have assembled here to fight in favour of Duryodhna. Hearing this, Lord Krishna placed the magnificent chariot in the middle of the battle field right in front of Bhishma and Drona and other kings in Kaurava's army. Seeing all his own people assembled in the battle field, desirous to fight, Arjun got overwhelmed with compassion, his body started trembling, mouth became dry and he started feeling loss of strength in his limbs. In this condition, he told Krishna that my mind is confused, I am unable to stand and the bow Gandeev is slipping out of my hand. I see bad omens also and do not find any good in killing my own people. I do not want kingdom or comforts since there will be no use of pleasures and enjoyment without my own family men and well wishers who have assembled here. How can I raise my bows and arrows and kill my teachers, paternal uncles, grand fathers, maternal uncles and other relatives and so on? I do not want to kill these people even for the kingdom of three worlds much less for the kingdom of this earth. By destroying these people, we will incur only sin. I would prefer to be unarmed and killed by Dhritrashtra's sons rather than killing them, since we cannot be happy by killing our own people.

Even though, these people overpowered by greed, do not see the defect in destruction of one's own family, but we know the sin involved in this destruction and therefore, why we should not withdraw from the dreadful war?

Arjun further explained the evils of the war saying that when the family is destroyed, the ancient family traditions and codes of moral conduct are also lost. When family traditions are destroyed, immortality takes over in the family. When immortality prevails, the women in the family will become corrupted, which will create complete confusion in the society. This will lead all of us to hell because the spirits of their ancestors are degraded when deprived of their post death rituals. The everlasting family traditions would be ruined by wrong actions of those who destroy the family, producing confusion with respect to family dharma, caste traditions and even the life dharma and so on. We have been told that people whose family traditions are destroyed necessarily dwell in hell for a long time. Alas! We are ready to commit a great sin by striving to slay our relatives because of greed for the pleasures of the kingdom. It would be far better for me if my cousin brothers kill me with their weapons in battle while I am unarmed and unresisting.

Having spoken in this manner, Arjun, with his mind completely under sorrow, kept aside his bow and arrows and sat down on the back seat of the chariot.

HARI OM –
Thus ends the first chapter entitled "Arjun Vishad Yog"

Do your duty with the attitude of Karm Yoga

- Surrender the fruits of your actions to Parmatma
- Find contentment in the journey you are on regardless of the outcome
- Whatever we do in the course of our lifetime should be dedicated to the Supreme Being remembering Him in any form - Krishna or Rama.
- This will always result in giving us peace and satisfaction and will make us feel God's presence with us all the time, making all our actions turn out to be positive.

CHAPTER 2 – THE KNOWLEDGE OF THE SELF

The teaching in Gita starts from verse 11 of chapter 2. Till that verse, Gita was dealing with sorrow of Arjun, sorrow caused to him by mere thought of losing his near and dear ones. And Krishna started giving this knowledge of the self and that of Nishkam Karm Yog only after Arjun prostrated in front of Shri Krishna and requested him to teach him what is best for him to do since he said that I do not want to fight this battle even if I get the kingdom of Swarg lok, what to talk of this kingdom on the earth. In first 10 shlokas of chapter 2, Arjun said very clearly that he would prefer to become a Sanyasi and get his food by alms rather than enjoy the wealth and power by killing his own people. Therefore, finding Arjun in this great sorrow and depression and accepting him his disciple, Shri Krishna started giving the divine teaching in the middle of the battle field itself. Thus the teachings of the Gita begin with the true knowledge of the self and the physical body from verse 11.

Krishna tells Arjun that he should not grieve for those who should not be grieved for. *'A wise person is one who does not grieve for one who is alive or the one who is dead.'*

Concept of Atma – Verse 11 to 15

The verse 11 in fact identifies the subject matter of Gita, bringing the concept of 'Jeev' as Atma. We all know that death of a person known to us is a cause of sadness, sorrow. The extent of sorrow depends upon how close you were to that person or how much you loved him. Krishna says, your sorrow or grief is not going to resolve the problem. One who is born, has to die one day and one who dies, will take birth again in different form or body. What is subject to change will change in any case. But Atma is constant; it always existed and will always remain same, and is not subject to change at all. **ATMA IS THE TRUTH.** Just as nature of water is not affected by the wave, the nature of Atma is SAT CHIT ANAND. Shri Krishna thus explains to Arjun that the entity that we call the "self" is really the Atma, not the material body, and is eternal, just as God himself is eternal. And thus establishes the principle of transmigration of the soul from lifetime to lifetime.

The human body undergoes three stages of childhood, adulthood and old age but in each stage, the self or Atma remains the same. Similarly, at the time of death, the Atma passes into another body. The death and birth are only for the body but Atma is never destroyed. Therefore, a wise person who knows the true nature of Atma does not sorrow over dead ones.

Our sense organs when come into contact with sensory objects, give us the experience of cold and heat, pleasure and pain, etc. However, these experiences keep on changing, when there is summer, we long for winter to come and when winter come, we start waiting for summer again. Also, some people feel better during summer while some feel miserable in summer. If you permit yourself to be affected by them, you will sway like a pendulum from side to side. A person of discrimination should practice to tolerate both the feelings of happiness and distress without being disturbed by them.

Shri Krishna tells Arjun that nothing is constant in this world except Atma which does not undergo any changes. The person, who is not affected by these heat and cold or pleasure and pain and remains same in all situations, becomes eligible for liberation. He accepts all situations happily and does not allow himself to be swayed by either pleasant situations or unpleasant situations. The phenomenal world cannot exist without the pairs of opposites - Good and evil will always exist and so too the pain and pleasure will always exist. The universe is a playground designed by God for the living entities. Both negative and positive experiences are needed for our growth and spiritual development. Cessation of pain brings pleasure and cessation of pleasure results in pain. Sorrow exists because the desire for happiness exists. When the desire for happiness disappears, so does the sorrow. Sorrow is only a prelude to happiness and vice versa. Even the joy of going to heaven is followed by the sorrow of coming back to the earth; therefore, worldly objects should not be the main goal of human life. If one chooses material pleasures, it is like giving up nectar and choosing poison instead.

Relationship between Atma and body (Verse 16 to 30)

The Atma; the soul, residing in every Physical Body is invisible and eternal, whereas the visible physical body is transitory, and it undergoes changes. The reality of these two is indeed certainly seen by the knower of the truth who knows that his real nature is not this body, but the Atma residing within the body.

This Atma pervades the whole body and is indestructible and no one can destroy the imperishable Atma. The body is made from inert matter and hence devoid of consciousness, while the Atma is sentient, i.e. it possesses consciousness. The Atma passes on the quality of consciousness to the body as well, by residing in it. Hence, the Atma pervades the body by spreading its consciousness everywhere in it, just like the fragrance of the flower pervades in the entire garden.

Only the physical bodies are perishable and get destroyed in time, while the Atma residing in each physical body is eternal, immutable, and incomprehensible. Therefore Shri Krishna asks Arjun that you must fight.

One who thinks that this Atma is a killer and one who thinks that the Atma can be killed, both are ignorant, because the Atma can never be destroyed and it does not cause any one to be destroyed.

The Atma is neither born, nor dies at any time. It does not come into being or cease to exist; it always exists. It is unborn, eternal, permanent, and primeval. The Atma is not destroyed when the body is destroyed. Therefore, an enlightened person who knows that the Atma is indestructible, eternal, unborn, and immutable, cannot kill anyone or cause anyone to be killed.

Lord Krishna tells Arjun that if you say that I sorrow over the dead bodies, this also is not right since just as a person gives up old cloths and puts on new garments, similarly, the individual Atma, gives up old bodies and acquires new bodies.

Weapons cannot cut this Atma, fire cannot burn it, water cannot make it wet, and the wind cannot make it dry. The Atma cannot be cut, burned, drowned, or dried. It is eternal, all pervading, changeless, immovable, and immemorial. Atma is beyond space and time. The Atma is said to be unexplainable, incomprehensible, and immutable. Knowing this as such, you should not grieve for the physical body.

Even if you think that the Atma takes birth and dies perpetually, even then, you should not grieve like this because death is certain for one who is born, and birth is certain for one who dies. Therefore, you should not lament over the inevitable death.

All beings are without any form or body or are invisible to our physical eyes, before birth and after death. They appear in a particular form or body between the birth and the death only. Therefore, what is there to grieve about?

It is very difficult to understand the science of Atma. Some look upon this Atma as a wonder, another describes it as a wonder and others hear of it as a wonder, but only very few people know its true nature. The Atma that dwells in the body of all living beings is eternally indestructible; therefore, one should not mourn or grieve for anybody.

Verse 31 to 37 – Krishna reminds Arjun of his duties as a warrior

After explaining the relationship between the Atma and the physical body and the real nature of Atma, Shri Krishna Asked Arjun to remember his duty as a warrior, and not to waver now at this stage, remembering that there is nothing more auspicious than doing one's own duties. Only the fortunate warriors get such an opportunity for a righteous war against evil, which has come to you by chance and which is like an open door to heaven. But if you will not engage in this battle which is in keeping with your Dharma, you will then fail in your duty, lose your reputation as a warrior, and incur sin. People will talk about your disgrace for a long time and for an honorable person like you, dishonour is worse than death. The great warriors will think that you have retreated from the battle out of fear. Those who held you in high esteem will stop respecting you. Your enemies will speak many unmentionable words and scorn your ability.

What could be more painful to you than this? If killed in the war, you will go to heaven or if victorious, you will enjoy the kingdom on the earth. Therefore, get up with a determination to fight.

Thus in verses 11 to 30, Krishna teaches Arjun the knowledge of Sankhy Yog or Gyan Yog, the nature of reality of Atma, whereas verses 31 to 37 are purely contextual and have nothing to do with the nature of Atma. These 7 verses are therefore not connected to the topic of Gyan Yoga being taught thus far. These verses just represent a particular argument from the stand point of one's duty or Dharma.

From verse 38 to 53, Shri Krishna introduces the topic of Karm Yog.

Shri Krishna introduces the topic of Karm Yog in verse 38 by asking Arjun to engage in performing your duty treating pleasure and pain, gain and loss, and victory and defeat to be the same. By doing your duty this way, you will not incur any sin. He thus advises Arjun to become detached from outcomes and simply focus on doing his duty. When he fights with the attitude of equanimity, treating victory and defeat, pleasure and pain as the same, then despite killing his enemies, he will never incur sin.

Krishna then says in verse 39 to Arjun that so far, I have imparted to you the wisdom with reference to Self-knowledge and now listen to the Karm Yoga, the Yog of doing selfless action, endowed with which you will free yourself from all **Karmik** bondage, or sin. In this verse Shri Krishna has called it *'Buddhi Yog'*, 'the Yog of the intellect', since only human beings have been endowed with the faculty of knowledge, for a higher purpose, so that they may utilize it to elevate themselves. The human birth is a rare opportunity and if one does not utilize it to achieve the higher goal, it is waste of human birth and one will continue in the circle of birth and death.

As human beings, our intellect possesses the ability to control the mind. Thus, we must cultivate the intellect with proper knowledge and use it to guide the mind in the proper direction. *'Buddhi Yog'* is the art of detaching the mind from the fruits of actions, by developing a resolute decision of the intellect that all work is meant for the pleasure of God. Such a person of resolute intellect cultivates single-minded focus on the goal, and traverses the path like an arrow released from the bow.

Every human being wants to gain Moksh (Attain everlasting happiness), and as we have seen in verses 11 - 30, Moksh can be gained through knowledge and to gain that knowledge, one requires a certain mind. Doing actions with a certain attitude will help one to prepare his mind to gain that knowledge. Karm Yog is an attitude, not just doing actions. But Karm Yog is doing the karmas with certain attitude for the sake of self purification. Lord Krishna is now going to talk about it in verses 40 to 53. Karm Yog has also been called Nishkam Karm Yog in these verses.

Importance of following the path of Karm Yog

In verse 40 & 41, Shri Krishna informs Arjun about the benefits of practicing Karm Yog. Bhagvaan says while doing Nishkam Karm Yog, no effort ever goes to waste and there is no adverse or opposite effect. Even a little practice of this discipline protects one from the great fear of the cycle of repeated birth and death. Shri Krishna is conveying here that once we commence on the journey of spiritual practice then even if we do not complete the path in this life, God preserves it and gives us the fruits in the next human life, enabling us to start off from where we had left.

A Karm Yogi has single minded determination only for God-realization; while a person who works for enjoyment of fruits of actions alone, has endless desires which make his mind running in many directions.

From verse 42 to 46, Krishna explains the results of Sakam Karm meaning performing rituals prescribed in Vedas

The Vedas are divided into three sections. These are: Karm-kāṇḍ (ritualistic ceremonies), gyān-kāṇḍ (knowledge section), and Upāsanā-kāṇḍ (devotional section). The Karm-kāṇḍ section advocates the performance of ritualistic ceremonies for material rewards and promotion to the celestial abodes. Those who seek sensual pleasures glorify this section of the Vedas.

Shri Krishna says that the misguided persons with limited understanding get attracted to the Karm-kand portion of Vedas which advocate practice of ostentatious (fancy) rituals for elevation to the heavenly abodes. They think that this is the whole purpose of the Vedas and there is no other higher principle of spiritual practice described in them. They are dominated by material desires and consider the attainment of heaven as the highest goal of life. Therefore, they perform many actions as well as spiritual rituals for the sake of fulfilling their desires, to gain material prosperity and enjoyment in this birth and the next birth. With their minds deeply attached to worldly pleasures, they engage their intellects in maximizing their enjoyment. Bewildered in this manner, they are unable to develop the firm determination required for success on the path of God-realization.

A portion of the Vedas deals with three qualities of goodness, passion, and ignorance, based on which the human beings perform actions to fulfill their desires and materialistic needs. Shri Krishna asks Arjun to rise above these three gunas and then do your duties as a **Karm Yogi. In this way,** one becomes free from pairs of opposites like sorrow and joy, victory and defeat and remains ever focused in self-knowledge. Therefore a person who remains steadfast in **Karm Yog**, and does not have any concern or anxiety for acquisition and preservation of material objects, is the master of oneself.

To the enlightened person, who has realized the true nature of the Atma within, that portion of Vedas is as useful as a small reservoir of water when the water of a huge lake becomes available. One who has realized the Supreme Being, will not desire the attainment of heaven mentioned as the fruits of performing Vedic rituals. Scriptures, such as the Vedas, are necessary means, but not the end. Scriptures are meant to lead and guide us on the spiritual path. Once the goal is reached, they have served their purpose.

Shri Krishna now describes theory and practice of Karm Yog in verse 47.

Shri Krishna says that your duty is to work only and not to the fruit thereof. You have choice of doing your Karmas but you have no choice or claim over its results. The fruits of work should not be your motive, and you should never be inactive.

This is an extremely popular verse of the Bhagavad Gita; it offers deep insight into the proper spirit of work and is often quoted whenever the topic of Karm Yog is discussed. The verse gives four instructions regarding the science of Karm Yog: 1) Do your duty, but do not concern yourself with the results. 2) You have choice of doing karmas but you have no choice over its results. 3) Fruit of work should not be your motive for doing your duty. 4) Do not be inactive as well.

It is true that we do actions (Karm) to fulfill our desire. Desires are of two types – Raag and Dvesh. **Raag** is what you want to have, what you want to retain and

Dvesh is what you want to avoid or get rid of. To do actions without expecting success or good results would be meaningless, but to be fully prepared for the unexpected should be an important part of any planning. The essence of **Karm Yog** is to do Karm just to please the Lord; mentally renouncing the fruits of all action; and let God take care of the results. Do your duty in life to the best of your ability without any regard for the personal enjoyment of the fruits of your work.

Every action would certainly produce a result, but what will be the result is not in our hands. The result could be more than what you expected, less than what you expected, and opposite to what you expected or exactly the same what you expected. One can never predict accurately the results of actions since we have limited power and knowledge. A farmer has control over how he works on his land, what seeds he sows, yet he has no control over the harvest. Also, he cannot expect harvest if he does not work on his land and does not sow the seeds properly, waters them adequately and protects the crop from all sorts of storms and insects etc.

All results are taken care of by certain laws, called "Laws of Karma" and those laws are not created by human being but by the creator himself, the Lord. Once it is recognized that the Lord is the author of the laws of karma, the results of actions also come from the Lord and with this attitude, the results become a **Prasad**. Therefore, a **Karm Yogi**, recognizing this fact, happily accepts every result of action as a **Prasad** from God and does not get affected whether the fruit is sweet or sour.

Krishna further says in verse 48; *"do your duty to the best of your ability, with your mind attached to the Lord, abandoning worry and selfish attachment to the results, and remaining calm in both success and failure"'*. This evenness of mind (samatv-bhaav) is called Yog that leads to the union with God.

Karm Yog is thus defined as doing one's duty while maintaining equanimity and evenness of mind under all circumstances and with dedication to the Lord.

Karm done with selfish motives is far inferior to that done with proper attitude of selfless service and with dedication to the Lord. Those who perform actions only to enjoy the fruits of their actions are called misers because they do not use their intellect wisely for the benefit of mankind. Therefore Shri Krishna asks Arjun in verse 49 to work for a higher cause of gaining true knowledge by detaching yourself from the fruits of your work and offering the fruits of work to God.

Endowed with sameness of mind, a **Karm Yogi** becomes free from both vice and virtue in this life itself. Therefore, one should commit to the pursuit of Karm Yog since a Karm yogi alone is proficient in performing actions. Shri Krishna uses the phrase *'yogaḥ karmasu kauśhalam'*; in verse 50, meaning that practice of Karm Yog makes one most skillful and proficient in his work.

Consider the example of a sincere surgeon who operates people. He performs his duty with equanimity, and is undisturbed irrespective of whether the patient survives or dies. This is because he is merely doing his duty unselfishly, to the best of his ability, and is not attached to the results. Hence, even if the patient dies while being operated upon, the surgeon does not feel guilty of murder. However, if the same surgeon's only child needs to be operated, he does not have the courage to do so, because in the case of his child, he gets attached to the result and he fears he will not be able to perform the operation skillfully. Therefore, the attachment to the results affects our performance adversely.

We should know that engaging in action with attachment to the fruits thereof can never result into everlasting happiness; instead it brings in more miseries in their life and thus binds them in the cycle of birth and death. A Karm yogi, whose intellect has become steadfast with spiritual knowledge, renounces attachment to the fruits of all actions with an attitude of offering it to God. In doing so, their actions become free from karmic reactions and attains a blissful divine state that is free from all afflictions and anguish and thus gets liberated from bondage to the cycle of life and death. *A Karm Yogi avoids what is not to be done but what has to be done is done properly with the attitude as an offering to the Lord.*

Shri Krishna further states that one, whose intellect is illumined with spiritual knowledge, develops dispassion and no longer seeks material sense pleasures, knowing them to be prelude of misery. Such a person then becomes indifferent to the Vedic rituals which are meant for attaining temporary celestial abodes.

Having talked mainly so far about **Karm Yoga** and self knowledge, Bhagvaan summed up everything and told Arjun in verse 53 that when your mind stays steady and firm in divine consciousness, you are not easily shaken by various means and ends mentioned in the Vedas, then you will be enlightened and attain the state of perfect Yog.

Verse 54 – Arjuna Question

Arjuna was still not very clear about what Shri Krishna had explained to him about the wise person having his mind steadfast in divine consciousness and firm in practice of Yog and therefore, asked Shri Krishna about the description of an enlightened person (sthita-dhīḥ) whose mind is steady (sthita-pragya) and who is situated in divine consciousness (samādhi-stha). How such a person speaks, how he sits, walks and how he behaves with others.

The answers to all of the above questions are given by Lord Krishna in the remaining verses of this chapter. Both the characteristics of a wise person and means for becoming a wise person are discussed.

Characteristics of enlightened person (verse 55 onwards)

When a person completely gives up all selfish desires and cravings as they appear in the mind, and is happy with oneself and within oneself, that person is said to be the enlightened person of steady mind and intellect.

The person whose mind is not affected by adversity, who does not crave pleasures, and who is completely free from longings, fear and anger (veet-raag-bhaya-krodhaḥ) is said to be the sage of steady wisdom who is firmly situated in divine consciousness (samādhi-stha). (*Adversities refer here the situations which are not under your control like earthquakes, lightning and storms etc which are absolutely natural phenomenon, which are beyond ones control. A wise person remains unperturbed in any of such situations.*)

The pleasures or sukha can come from one's sensory pleasures or from some external events. One who does not yearn for such pleasures; who has no attachment to these pleasures and who is neither delighted by good fortune nor dejected by distress and miseries, such a person is a sage with perfect knowledge. For the person who is not attached to anything, who does not rejoice on getting the desired results and does not get perturbed by the undesired situation, mind and intellect of such a person become steady.

When the person is able to completely withdraw the sense organs from their objects, just like a tortoise withdraws its limbs into the shell for protection from calamity, then the mind and intellect of such a person is considered established in divine wisdom. If you keep on fulfilling the desires of the senses, the desires will never get extinguished, just as offering oblations of butter in the fire does not extinguish it; instead, it makes the fire blaze even stronger. Therefore, an enlightened soul withdraws himself from the sense objects just as a tortoise protects itself by drawing its limbs and head inside its shell.

If a person abstains from sense enjoyment, his desire for sensual pleasures may fade away temporarily if the craving and longing of sense enjoyment remains within the mind. However, even this subtle craving also completely disappears for the wise person who has realized the Supreme Lord. (*Thus, Shri Krishna teaches in this verse 59 that the desires must be sublimated by knowledge instead of just suppressing them.*)

In verse 60, Shri Krishna says that indeed these senses are so powerful that they forcibly carry away the mind even when the person makes sincere efforts and strives for perfection. Then how one can keep his senses under control?

Shri Krishna answers this himself in next verse 61 saying that the senses can be kept under complete control only by keeping the mind completely absorbed in devotion to the God. Only then the mind of such a person becomes steadfast and is a wise person having perfect knowledge.

Unfulfilled desires are the cause of anger (verses 62 & 63)

When a person keeps thinking about sense objects, he develops attachment for the same. Desire for sense objects is born from attachment to sense objects. If desires are fulfilled, it gives rise to greed since desire is never eliminated by satiating it. However, if the fulfillment of desire is obstructed, it gives rise to anger.

Anger leads to clouding of judgment and when the intellect is clouded, it leads to bewilderment of memory. The person then forgets what is right and what is wrong, and flows along with the surge of emotions, making the mind senseless and impatient. This leads to destruction of intellect. And since the intellect is the internal guide, when it gets destroyed, the person is ruined meaning that the person behaves in an insane manner.

Peace and Happiness can be attained through control of senses and mind alone (Verse 64 to 68)

Whereas a disciplined person who has his mind under control, enjoys the sense objects with his sense organs under his control and free from attachment and aversions, attains tranquility. When the mind becomes tranquil, the person becomes fit for receiving grace of God.

Attachment and aversion are two sides of the same coin. Aversion is nothing but negative attachment or dislike.

Just as, in attachment, the object of attachment repeatedly comes to one's mind; similarly, in aversion, the object of hatred keeps popping into the mind. So attachment and aversion to material objects both have the same effect on the mind—they dirty it and pull it into the three modes of material nature. When the mind is free from both attachment and aversion, and is absorbed in devotion to God, one receives the grace of God and experiences His unlimited divine bliss.

Shri Krishna further says that by divine grace, God bestows his divine knowledge, divine love, and divine bliss upon the person. Thus all his sufferings come to an end and his mind becomes tranquil. In that state of internal fulfillment, the intellect of that person becomes firmly established in God.

However, a person who has not controlled the mind and senses can neither have a resolute intellect nor steady contemplation on God. For one who has not united the mind with God, there is no peace; and when there is no peace, there can be no happiness. *Here, Shri Krishna is conveying to the mankind that those who refuse to discipline the mind and senses and do not engage in devotion to God continue to suffer. Material desires are like an itching eczema, and the more we indulge in them, the worse they become. Therefore, one can never be truly happy as long as he keeps indulging in material desires.*

If the mind follows the roving senses, it can lead the intellect astray and rob the person of his peace and happiness, just as a strong wind takes away a small boat in the sea from its destination. *It is stated in Kaṭhopaniṣhad that God has made our five senses outward facing. Hence, they are automatically drawn towards their objects in the external world, and even one of the senses on which the mind focuses has the power to lead it astray.*

(The Deer are attached to sweet sounds and thus the hunter attracts them by melodious music and then kills them. Bees are attached to fragrance and while they suck its nectar, the flower closes at night, and they get trapped within it. Fish are trapped by the desire for eating, and they swallow the bait of the fishermen. Insects are drawn to light; and as they come too close to the fire, get burnt. In a similar way, if a person keeps running after material desires, he gets trapped in this cycle of birth and death and does not attain Happiness.)

Therefore, Shri Krishna concludes in verse 68 that the mind and intellect of a person becomes steady only when his senses are completely withdrawn from sense objects and thus gets firmly established on the path of divine wisdom.

Material enjoyment is not the real purpose of life for wise people **(verses 69 – 72)**

In verses 69, Shri Krishna states "What all beings consider as day is the night of ignorance for the wise, and what all creatures see as night is the day for the yogi.

Let us try and understand the true meaning of these words. Shri Krishna is conveying here to Arjun that those who are ignorant of the true nature of the Self look to material enjoyment as the real purpose of life. They consider the opportunity for worldly pleasures as the success of life, or consider it as their day and deprivation from sense pleasures as darkness, or consider it as night for them. On the other hand, a person with divine knowledge sees sense enjoyment as harmful for the soul, and hence views it as night. They also consider refraining from the objects of the senses as elevating to the soul, and hence look on it as day. Using those connotations of the words, Shri Krishna states that what is night for the wise, is day for the worldly-minded people, and vice versa.

Just as waters from all rivers from all directions keep flowing into the ocean but the ocean remains undisturbed by the incessant flow of water, in a similar way, the realized yogi remains calm and unmoved in both conditions; while utilizing sense objects for bodily necessities, or being bereft of them. Only such a person attains shanti, or true peace.

One who desires material objects does not gain peace. Trying to fulfill material desires is like adding more wood to the fire. The fire will go out if no more wood is added to it, similarly only that person attains peace who has abandoned his attachment and longings for all desires. He attains peace who lives in this world without the sense of doer ship giving up his ego and does not consider himself as owner of anything.

Shri Krishna concludes this chapter by telling Arjun that an enlightened person having reached the state of Brahm-sthiti (known as God-realization of divine consciousness) is immediately liberated from delusion of Maya for the rest of eternity. This state is also called jeevan mukt meaning that the soul is liberated even when residing in the body. Remaining in this state of divine consciousness, at the time of death, the soul finally discards the corporeal body, gets liberated from the cycle of birth and death and finally reaches the Supreme Abode of God. *(This state of eternal liberation from Maya is also called nirvaaṇ, moksha, etc.)*

- **HARI OM -**

Thus ends the second chapter entitled "Sankhya Yog

CHAPTER 3 - PATH OF SELFLESS SERVICE

Arjun had made very clear in the beginning of second chapter that he wanted liberation, **Moksh**. He also told Krishna "I am your student; please teach me so that I can gain the best - the **Moksh**. In response to that, Krishna told him about the nature of Atma and told him that knowledge of Atma alone will provide him liberation. Bhagvaan Krishna also described the qualities of a wise person who has this knowledge. Krishna told him that a wise person is one who gives up all his desires and remains happy with oneself in oneself. Arjun therefore understood that in order to gain liberation, he should renounce all his activities, take Sanyas and live his life to gain knowledge.

However, in verse 2.48, Krishna asked Arjun to perform action, remaining rooted in Karm Yog and also told him briefly what Karm Yog is. Arjun still understood that if I perform Karm, I will be bound by results of actions and therefore Karm Yog is not adequate for gaining liberation. But Lord Krishna again asked him to get up and fight with the spirit of Karm Yog. Arjuna was thus confused and did not know whether he should do his duties as a warrior and fight the war or renounce all activities and take Sanyas to gain knowledge. To clear this doubt, Arjun, therefore asked a question from Shri Krishna and this is how the third chapter begins with Arjun's question in first two verses.

Arjun's Question in verse 1 & 2

Arjun asked Shri Krishna; "If you consider that acquiring knowledge is better than actions, then why do you want me to do actions and indulge in this horrible war. You seem to confuse my mind by apparently conflicting words. Please tell me, decisively, one thing by which I shall gain liberation."

Therefore, Shri Krishna expounds further on Karm Yog or the Yog of action in this chapter from verse 3 onwards.

Karm Yog is preferred life style than Sanyas (Verse 3 - 9)

In verse 3, Lord Krishna said that in the previous chapter (verse 2.39) and in the past also, he had explained two paths leading to enlightenment - the path of knowledge (known as Sankhy Yog) for those inclined toward contemplation, and the path of selfless actions (known as Karm Yog or Buddhi Yog) for those inclined toward action.

One does not gain the state of actionless-ness by merely giving up all activities, nor does he gain liberation by renouncing the world and becoming a Sanyasi. Mere abstinence from physical work does not result in a state of freedom from karmic reactions. Also the true knowledge does not get awakened by renouncing the world as long as the mind remains impure.

One cannot exist even for a moment without action because everyone is forced to perform action helplessly by the three qualities of Satv, rajas and Tamas born of nature.

Anyone who outwardly pretends to have controlled his senses but mentally keeps thinking of the sense pleasures is called a hypocrite and just trying to befool others. Shri Krishna is conveying here that running away from the problems of life by prematurely taking Sanyas is not the way forward in the journey of the evolution of the soul. In fact, without true knowledge, no one can renounce all activities. Whereas, those who are unattached and keeping his sense organs and mind under control, engage the organs of actions in Karm Yog , are far superior. Therefore, perform actions which are to be done as your duty because remaining in activity is indeed far better than sitting idle. Even the maintenance of your body would be impossible without doing actions.

It is also not wise to abandon activities due to the fear of getting bound by the results of those actions, because one gets bound by only those actions which are not done as an offering to the Lord. Therefore, do your duty as a service to God for the good of humanity and you will not be bound by results of your actions.

Why it is essential to do all works as sacrifice to God? (Verse 10 - 13)

While fulfilling your household duties, perform all works as a sacrifice to God, who is the Enjoyer of all fruits of actions. Such people, though living in the world, never get bound by their actions.

In the beginning of creation, Brahma created humankind along with their respective duties and had told all human beings; "May you multiply by doing all services to various gods and these gods shall fulfill all your desires. Nourish the celestial gods with selfless service, and these gods pleased by selfless service with give you the desired results. Thus nourishing one another, you shall attain the Supreme goal."

Shri Krishna further says that one who enjoys the gift given by these gods, without sharing with others is indeed a thief. Because the wise people who eat the food after sharing with others are freed from all sins while the selfish people who cook food only for themselves without first offering to gods or sharing with others, in fact, eat sin only.

In these verses Shri Krishna has conveyed the importance of maintaining the cosmic ecology and not to disturb the same by not doing what is to be done. All the elements of nature including all gods and living creatures are integral parts of the system of God's creation. The sun lends stability to the earth and provides heat and light necessary for life to exist. Earth creates food from its soil for our nourishment and also holds essential minerals in its womb for a civilized lifestyle. The air moves the life force in our body and enables transmission of sound energy. The air that we breathe in, the Earth that we walk upon, the water that we drink, and the light that illumines our day, are all gifts of creation to us. While we partake of these gifts to sustain our lives, we also have our duties toward the integral system. Shri Krishna says that we are obligated to participate with the creative force of nature by performing our prescribed duties in the service of God. That is the sacrifice or yagya He expects from us. (The word Yagya mentioned here has wider meaning. Yagya as per Vedic scriptures, generally means a sacrificial ritual where we offer various things like ghee, food etc in the fire. In a wider sense, it means every action of one's life should be performed as an offering to the Lord.)

However, if we begin looking upon the gifts of nature, not as means of serving the Lord but as objects of our own enjoyment, Shri Krishna calls it a stealing mentality. The world that we live in is created by God, and everything in it belongs to him. Just as if we go to someone's house whom we do not know and take away something without the knowledge of the house owner, it is considered as a theft in the eyes of law. Similarly, if we utilize His creation for our pleasures, without acknowledging His dominion over it and do not give back something in return to maintain the balance, from the divine perspective we are certainly committing theft. Those who cook food for themselves become implicated in the sin. But doing it as a yagya or sacrifice to the Lord, nullifies the sinful reactions. Let's not disturb the cosmic ecology.

Cycle of Nature; verse 14 - 17

In the same context, Shri Krishna says that all the living beings are sustained from food; food is produced by rain and rain is produced by yagya or sacrifices and **yagyas are** done by human beings by performing their duties.

Actions and duties are prescribed in the Vedas and Vedas have come from the eternal Lord. Thus the all-pervading Supreme Being, the God is ever present in sacrifices (yagyas) of human being.

We humans are the only ones in this chain who have been bestowed with the ability to choose our actions by our own free will. We can thus either contribute to the harmony of the cycle by performing our duties in accordance with the divine laws or bring about discord in the smooth running of this cosmic mechanism by becoming slaves to our senses.

A person who does not live in his life, according to the wheel of creation already set in motion and rejoices in sense pleasures only, that sinful person lives in vain. But persons conforming to the divine law become pure at heart and free from material contamination.

A self-realized soul is not obliged to perform any duty (verse 17 & 18)

The person who rejoices only within self, who is delighted in the self, and who is contented in the self alone, for such a Self-realized person there is no work to be done. For him, there is no purpose here in this world for doing or not doing any Vedic rituals. (*The Vedas are there to help unite the self with the Supreme Self. When God-realization takes place, the task of the Vedas is over. Such an enlightened soul is no longer obliged to perform the Vedic rituals.*)

Such self-realized souls have nothing to gain or lose either in performing their duties or renouncing all works. Nor do they need to depend on other living beings to fulfill their self-interest.

Shri Krishna recommends Arjun to be a Karm yogi (verse 19 - 21)

Shri Krishna recommends Arjun in verse 19 to always perform actions efficiently and with a selfless motive without any attachment to the results of actions, which also lead a person to attain the supreme goal of life.

King Janaka and many others have gained liberation by performing actions alone without getting attached to the results of actions. Therefore, Shri Krishna advises Arjun that you should also perform your duties with a view to guide people and for the welfare of society, because whatever noble persons do, others follow. Whatever standard they set up, the world follows.

Even a Gyani should continue doing his duties (Verse 22-29)

Lord Krishna further tells Arjun that there is nothing in the three worlds (heaven, earth, and the lower regions) that needs to be done by Me, nor there is anything which is not accomplished by me that I should accomplish, still I engage in actions.

If I do not engage in actions carefully, people would follow the same path in every way. If I were not to perform actions, these worlds would perish, and I would be the cause of confusion and destruction of human beings.

Just as the ignorant people do actions with attachment to the fruits of actions for themselves, in a similar way the wise should also do actions without attachment to the fruits of actions, for the sake of leading people on the right path. The wise person should not create any disturbance in the minds of the ignorant, who are attached to the fruits of actions, but should inspire others by performing all actions efficiently without selfish attachment.

Lord further says in verse 27 that in fact, all actions are performed in various ways by the forces of Prakriti (i.e. three modes of material nature), but due to delusion, the ignorant people think themselves to be the doer. Whereas the person who knows the truth about the role of the forces of Prakriti in getting the actions done, does not get bound by the results of actions, since he knows that the senses, mind and organs of actions engage themselves with reference to their respective objects. But those who come under the spell of Maya (the forces of Prakriti), become attached to their actions. Shri Krishna says that the wise person should not disturb the mind of those who are ignorant and whose knowledge is imperfect and therefore, let them continue doing their work in accordance with their desires.

Karm Yog is the path to get rid of Bondage of actions (verses 30- 32)

After explaining the Karm Yog in this way, **Shri Krishna asks Arjun to do your prescribed duty, with a spiritual frame of mind, free from expectations of gaining any materialistic objects, without any complaints whatsoever and fight.** Those who always constantly practice this teaching of mine with faith and tolerance, become free from the bondage of Karma. Whereas those who criticize this teaching without any reason and do not follow my vision, are to be considered ignorant, senseless, and confused.

Do your duty keeping Likes and Dislikes under control (verse 33-34)

Bhagvaan further tells Arjun in verse 33 that all beings follow their nature. Even the wise person acts according to his own nature. Therefore, there is no use to even try to go against your own nature. All sense organs have Attachments and aversions for the objects, some sense objects attract the sense organs towards them while some create aversion. A person should not come under the control of these two because they are two major stumbling blocks, on the path towards Self-realization.

Do your natural duty following your Dharma; verse 35

In this verse, Shri Krishna says that it is far better to perform one's natural prescribed duty, even though it may be inferior or tinged with faults, than to perform somebody else prescribed work how so ever good or well performed it may be. In fact, it is preferable to die in the discharge of one's duty, than to follow the path of another, which is fraught with danger.

In this verse, the word dharma has been used in two contexts - svadharma and pardharma. There is no exact translation of word Dharma in English. Terms like righteousness, good conduct, duty, noble quality, etc. only describe one aspect of its meaning. Dharma comes from the root word dhṛi, which means ḍhāraṇ karane yogya, or "duties and actions that are appropriate for us."

For example, the dharma of a son is to respect his parents.

The svadharma is our personal dharma, which is the dharma applicable to our context, situation, maturity, and profession in life. Pardharma is the dharma of others applicable to their nature, profession. This svadharma can change as our context in life changes, and as we grow spiritually. For example, as a student his svadharma is to study diligently and as a householder, his svadharma is to do work in accordance with his nature and qualification following the right path for bringing up his family. He should not change the work simply because someone else may be doing something else and earning much more than him.

The duties born of our nature can be easily performed with stability of mind. The duties of others may seem attractive from a distance and we may think of switching, but that is a risky thing to do. If they conflict with our nature, they will create disharmony in our senses, mind, and intellect. Shri Krishna emphasizes this point dramatically by saying that it is better to die in the faithful performance of one's duty than to be in the unnatural position of doing another's duty.

Arjun question – verse 36

Arjun knew that sometimes a man commits sin unknowingly and therefore asked Krishna; "what impels one to commit a sin or selfish deeds as though by force even if one does not wish to go against one's will".

The question asked by Arjun is very realistic and representative of the human struggle. We all have a conscience that makes us feel remorseful while committing a sin. We all know that stealing, swindling, extortion; murder, oppression, and corruption are all sinful activities. But, yet we commit such acts, as if some external strong force impels us to do them. Arjun wishes to know what that strong force is.?

Desire (lust) and Anger are the force behind this (Verse 37- 39)

Lord Krishna said that it is 'lust' (desire for worldly enjoyments), born out of passion which drives human beings towards committing sins. When desire is satisfied, it becomes greed and when desire is not satisfied, it gives rise to anger. Greed is insatiable; it never gets completely fulfilled and is a great devil. Greed is nothing but intensified desire, while anger is frustrated desire. Hence, Shri Krishna labels lust, or desire, as the root of all evils. One commits sin under the influence of these three – desire, greed and anger.

(In verse 37, Shri Krishna in fact has described kaam and krodh as the root cause of all sinful acts by human beings. The word kaam in Vedic terms is used not only for sexual desires but also for all sorts of desires for worldly enjoyments including the urge for money,

prestige, power and physical cravings, etc. Greed (Lobh) and anger (krodh) arise from desires only as described above)

Just as the fire is covered by cloud of smoke; just as the reflective power of a mirror is masked by dust, and just as an embryo is concealed by the womb, similarly, the knowledge; discriminatory ability of the intellect of the person gets covered by this insatiable fire of desire. Shri Krishna states that it is the insatiable and inexhaustible desires that are responsible for shrouding the power of discrimination of even the wise person and therefore one should know them to be root of all miseries and eternal enemy. Desires burn like unquenchable fire and never brings happiness to anyone.

Method of controlling desire and anger; verse 40 - 43

Shri Krishna now describes how one should control the senses to restrain desires or lust. Bhagvaan says, the senses, the mind, and the intellect are said to be the seat of lust. Under the sway of lust, the sense objects are desired by the senses, the senses infatuate the mind, the mind misleads the intellect, and the intellect loses its discriminatory powers. When the intellect is clouded, the human being is deluded to become a slave of lust and will do anything to satiate it.

Therefore, Shri Krishna tells Arjun to control the senses in the beginning itself and kill this devil of material desires residing in them, which destroys intellect and wisdom. *To accomplish this, Shri Krishna tells Arjun to use his higher instrument given to us by God.*

Shri Krishna then describes that the gross physical body is made of gross matter; therefore, the five sense organs which are in the subtle body, are superior to it (which grasp the perceptions of taste, touch, sight, smell, and sound). The mind is superior to the senses because it is subtler than the sense organs. The intellect having the ability to discriminate is even more subtle and therefore superior to the mind; and the Self, the Atma, which is subtler than the subtle, is superior to the intellect.

Thus, knowing the Atma to be the highest and strongest, control your senses, mind and intellect and destroy this mighty enemy in the form of lust (desire and greed) with the sword of true knowledge of the Self.

This has been beautifully explained in the Upanishads with the example of a chariot pulled by five horses with the help of reins in their mouth which are in the hands of a charioteer; and a passenger (The individual soul) sitting at the back of the chariot. In this analogy, the chariot is the body, the horses are the five senses, the reins in the mouth of the horses is the mind, and the charioteer is the intellect.

Ideally, the passenger instructs the charioteer, who then controls the reins and guides the horses in the proper direction. However if the passenger (individual soul) goes to sleep, the charioteer does not know where to go and so it is not able to guide the horses with the help of reins which direction to go. In a similar way, in the materially bound state, the bewildered person (the passenger sitting at the back of the charioteer) does not direct the intellect in the proper direction. Thus, the senses decide the direction where the chariot will go. In this way a human being is moving around in the material world since eternity.

However, if the person (the individual soul) wakes up to his higher nature; the soul true nature of Sat-Chit-Anand and decides to take a proactive role, it can exercise the intellect in the proper direction. The intellect will then govern the mind and mind thus controls the senses to move in the direction of eternal bliss. In this way, the higher self (soul) must be used to control the lower self (senses, mind, and, intellect).

- HARI OM –

Thus ends Third chapter entitled "KARMYOG"

KARM YOG IN SHORT

- Do not be slave to your desires
- Do not get attached to your desires
- Have evenness of mind in all situations even when your desires are not fulfilled
- The results of actions is not in your hands and you have no control over it
- Accept the results of actions as Prasad of Bhagvaan

CHAPTER 4 - PATH OF RENUNCIATION WITH KNOWLEDGE

Lord Krishna started teaching Arjun in the middle of the battle field, when Arjun was confused and in despair and when he no longer wanted to fight. In Chapter 2 itself, Krishna had imparted the entire teaching, talking about knowledge first and then about Karm Yog, how one should live his life doing his duties without getting attached to the fruits of actions. At the end of Chapter 2, Krishna also described the qualities of a wise person having this knowledge, how he sits, how he talks and what are his attitudes while doing his duties, his actions. The teachings continued further from Chapter 3 since Arjun was not sure whether he should indulge in gaining this knowledge or engage in his duties to fight the war to regain his kingdom. Therefore in Chapter 3, Krishna explains in details about Karm Yog and asked Arjun to do his duties with the attitude of Karm Yog.

In first three verses of Fourth chapter, Lord Krishna told Arjun that this knowledge of eternal science of Yog is not something new, but it was disclosed in the beginning of creation by me, (Krishna himself), to Vivasvan, or Surya, the Sun God, who imparted it to Manu, the original progenitor of humankind; Manu in turn taught it to Ikshvaku, first king of the Solar dynasty. In this way, it has been handed down from generation to generation. But with long lapse of time, this knowledge got forgotten and that's why I am giving you the same ancient knowledge because you are my devotee and my dear friend. This particular knowledge is a great secret because it can be gained only when someone is prepared to gain it and understand it.

Now Arjun had a doubt and therefore asked Shri Krishna that how can I understand that you taught this knowledge yourself at the beginning of creation; since Sun was born in ancient times much long before you were born.

Incarnation of God to establish Dharma (Verse 5- 10)

To clear Arjun's doubt, Lord Krishna said that both you and I have taken many births. I remember them all, but you do not remember. *(Shri Krishna thus emphasizes here in this verse the difference between the individual soul (Arjun) and God (Lord Krishna) by stating that although the God descends in the world innumerable times, He still remains omniscient and all knowing, unlike the individual soul whose knowledge is finite, who knows only about that body in which it resides.)*

Shri Krishna further says that even though, I am unborn, and lord of all beings, I am imperishable, yet I come into human form from time to time, by my own divine power (Yogmaya). *In this verse, Shri Krishna has conveyed that although the God is formless, He manifests in a personal form by virtue of his own divine power called Yogmaya.*

When and why he manifests in human form; he answers this question by himself in next two verses 7 &

8. When He takes avatar, is explained in verse 7 and why He takes avatar, is explained in verse 8.

Whenever there is a decline of Righteousness (or decline of Dharma) or there is increase of unrighteousness (adharma), I manifest myself in human form on this earth from time to time.

I appear on this earth age after age, in order to protect the good people (saints and sadhus), to transform or destroy the wicked and criminal minded people and for reestablishing the principles of Dharma. Shri Krishna has thus described here three main purpose of His incarnation on the earth.

The One, who truly understands My divine birth and My pastimes in this way, attains My Supreme Abode and is not born again after leaving this body.

Bhagvaan further says that after being freed from attachment, fear, and anger, becoming fully absorbed in Me, and taking refuge in Me, many persons in the past have became purified by the knowledge of the Supreme Lord, and have attained My divine love.

In fact, attachment is the cause of both fear and anger. Fear arises out of apprehension that the object of our attachment, which we like, will be snatched away from us. And anger arises when there is an obstruction in attaining the object of our attachment. Attachment is thus the root cause of the mind getting dirty. Instead, when we *absorb the same mind in God, such devotion purifies the mind. Thus, the sovereign recipe to cleanse the mind from the defects of lust, anger, greed, envy, and illusion, is to detach it from the worldly objects and attach it to the **Supreme Lord.***

The law of Karma (verse 11 – 15)

Shri Krishna now explains the law of Karma -" you get according to your karmas as per divine laws set by God". Lord Krishna states that He reciprocates with everyone in same way as they surrender to Him. With whatever motive people worship Me, I fulfill their desires accordingly. God sitting in the hearts of every human being keeps notes of all their actions and thoughts and dispenses the results according to the laws of Karma set forth by Him. Everyone has to follow these laws knowingly or unknowingly.

Those who want to enjoy the materialistic world in this life itself, worship the celestial gods, because in this way they get the results of their actions very quickly. But they don't know that these material gains are given by the celestial gods by virtue of the power they have received from the Supreme Lord only.

Shri Krishna says that I created the four-fold divisions of human society based on their qualities and duties. Though I am the author of this system, one should know that I, being eternal, am the non-doer of this, since I do nothing directly.

(As an example the nature of fire is to burn but it will burn only if you put your finger in the fire. Therefore, it is not fire which burnt your finger but it got burnt because you put it inside the fire. Rain is another similar example. Just as rain water falls equally on the forest, yet from some seeds huge banyan trees sprout, from other seeds beautiful flowers bloom, and from some others, thorny bushes emerge. The rain, which is impartial, is not answerable for this difference. Therefore, as fire is non-doer, as rain is non-doer directly, in a similar way, although God created the four-fold groups of people based on their qualities and duties, God is the non-doer and it is the human being who made it based on the birth.)

Shri Krishna again says that whatever work I do, these do not bind me because I have no desire for the fruits of actions. One who fully understands and practices this truth is also not bound by Karma. *(God is all pure and pure personalities are never tainted by defects even if they come in contact with impure situations and entities. The sun is pure and does not get tainted if sunlight falls on a dirty puddle of water, the sun always retains its purity while also purifying the dirty puddle. The fire is also pure, and whatever we pour into it also gets purified. Likewise, God is not tainted by any of the activities he performs.)*

Actions bind one in karmic reactions only when they are performed with the mentality of enjoying the results. Knowing this truth, even seekers of liberation in ancient times performed actions. Therefore, Shree Krishna advises Arjun to perform your duty following the footsteps of those ancient sages.

The secret science of action (Verses 16 – 23)

Shri Krishna further says that it is very difficult to understand what is action and what is inaction. Even the wise are confused about it. Lord Krishna now reveals to Arjun the most secret science of action and inaction knowing which one gets liberated from the evil of birth and death. A Karm yogi is not subject to the Karmic laws.

Shri Krishna says that work can be divided into three categories; recommended action (Karm), forbidden action (vikarm), and inaction (akarm). The truth about these three is profound and difficult to understand.

Let's first define these three categories:

Action (Karm) - Any action that is done with the attitude of doer ship and for the purpose of enjoying the fruits of actions is called Karm in Gita. Karm bind us with the world.

Inaction (Akaram) – The dictionary meaning of inaction is "absence of action". In Physical science, action takes place only when there is movement involved. However, in Vedic philosophy, Akaram is the Karm that is done without selfish motive and without attachment to the fruits of actions. These actions do not bind the person to the world but liberate one from the cycle of birth and death. Therefore, inaction is those actions which are devoid of pride and done with the attitude of surrendering the results of actions to God. For example, if we do any ritual without any desire to get something in return for ourselves or we work for welfare of the mankind like providing food to the hungry without any selfish motive, then these actions are considered to be inaction, or virtuous act which helps in liberation.

Prohibited action (Vikarma) - *The actions which are prohibited and against Dharma are called Vikarm in Upanishad. Actions such as stealing or deceitful fraud or to torture someone for selfish gains etc. are sinful acts.*

In verse 18, Shri Krishna states that a person, who sees 'inaction in action' and 'action in inaction', is truly a wise person. Such a person is a yogi who has accomplished everything and there is nothing else to be done by him. Even the wise people call him a sage who does all actions without any desires (desire for fruit of actions) and who has burnt all his actions by the fire of self knowledge.

Let's understand what is the meaning of seeing 'action in inaction' and seeing 'inaction in action':

'seeing action in inaction'

Even when we are sitting idle and not doing any work with our organs of actions, but our sense organs and mind keep doing their functions. The mind is always having endless flow of thoughts even though we may not take physical action according to those thoughts. A learned person sees 'action in inaction' since he knows that all his sense organs and mind are performing actions at all times. Even opening or closing of eyes, breathing etc are all actions for a learned person. Just as a person does not perform any karma in the state of sleep, but a wise person knows that karma is being done in even in sleep, our breath keeps going and the soul is witness to all these actions even in the state of sleep.

'Seeing inaction in action'

When a person realizes that he is not the doer of any Karm, then the Karm done by him is not Karm but becomes akarm, because those actions do not bind the person to this world. He knows that whatever is happening in this world is because of Prakriti, the material nature. Further, any action which is done with the attitude of surrendering to the Lord becomes inaction because those actions are not the cause of material bondage and liberates the person from the cycle of birth and death.

Thus, it is the state of the mind that determines what is inaction and action. The minds of enlightened persons are always absorbed in God. Therefore, such people, having given up attachment to the fruits of their actions, are always satisfied and are not dependent on any of the external things. He does not do anything even though fully engaged in activity.

Such person free from all expectations, and free from sense of ownership of all possessions, having mastered his mind and senses, does not incur sin even though performing all actions by his body. All actions done by such a person are to sustain his body only. Their every act is performed with the divine intention of pleasing God. Content with whatever gain comes of its own accord, and free from envy, they remain unaffected by pairs of opposites such as likes and dislikes. Being equipoised in success and failure, they are not bound by their actions, even while performing all kinds of activities.

Lord Krishna then summarizes the conclusion of the previous seven verses. "They are released from the bondage of material attachments with their mind and intellect firmly rooted in divine knowledge. Since they perform all actions as a service to the almighty, they are freed from all karmic reactions." For such a wise person, every action is a holy sacrifice, a holy act, he perceives Lord in every action and he becomes one with the Lord upon attaining Moksh.

Krishna then describes twelve different types of spiritual practices or sacrifices in Verses from 24 to 33.

Verse 24 of chapter 4 is very important and famous shloka of Bhagavad-Gita. Shri Krishna says; "The wise persons, who have gained self knowledge, perform rituals knowing that all offerings are for the Lord, what is offered also goes to the Lord, the fire in which it is offered is also Lord, and he who is doing the rituals is also Lord himself."

It has a very deep meaning which is very essential to understand it clearly.

All the beings in the world are made from the material energy of God. The soul residing in every one is the spiritual energy of God called consciousness or jeev-shakti also. Just as the Sun and sun-rays are one as well as distinct from each other, in a similar way, the individual soul is also simultaneously one with the God and also different from God. Hence, those whose minds are fully absorbed in God-consciousness see the whole world in its unity with God as non-different from Him. He sees God everywhere and in all beings. For him, the person making the sacrifice, the object of the sacrifice, the instruments of the sacrifice, the sacrificial fire, and the act of sacrifice, are all perceived as non-different from God.

Having explained the spirit in which sacrifice is to be done, Lord Krishna now relates the different kinds of sacrifice people perform in this world for purification.

- There are some yogis who worship the celestial gods (like Indra, Varun, Agni, Moon and Sun etc.) with material offering to them.

- Then there are others having knowledge of deeper meaning of yagya, offer their own self as sacrifice in the fire of the Supreme Truth. This is called Atma samarpaṇ, or offering one's soul to God, meaning that they surrender themselves completely to God.
- Some others offer hearing and other senses in the sacrificial fire of restraint. They withdraw their mind completely from the senses by their will-power and give up their sensual pleasures. It is called 'haṭha Yog'.
- Still others offer objects of sense - sound, touch, smell, taste and Form as sacrifice in the fire of the senses. For them, the senses no longer remain as instruments for material enjoyment; rather they are sublimated to perceive God in everything. This is called practice of Bhakti Yog.
- There are some yogis who follow the path of discrimination, and offer all the activities of the senses, mind, intellect and organs of actions unto the fire of self knowledge, meaning that they always keep their mind focused on the supreme Lord. *(While haṭha yogis strive to restrain the senses by force of their will-power, the gyān yogis accomplish the same goal with the repeated practice of discrimination based on knowledge.)*
- Some perform 'Dravya yagya'. They are inclined toward earning wealth and donating it in charity toward a divine cause. They offer their tendency for earning money as sacrifice to God in devotion.

- There are others who offer severe austerities as sacrifice. They lead a life of prayerful discipline and practice 'tapah' in their devotion to God.
- Some practice the eight-fold path of yogic practices called aṣhṭāṅg Yog, for spiritual advancement, starting with physical techniques and ending in conquest of the mind. They offer their yogic practice as yagya in the fire of devotion.
- Others study the scriptures and cultivate knowledge as sacrifice, while observing strict vows to follow the life of discipline and studies.
- There are those who engage in yogic practices of reaching the breathless state by offering inhalation into exhalation and exhalation into inhalation as a sacrifice (by using short breathing Kriya techniques).
- Some arduously practice prāṇāyām and restrain the incoming and outgoing breaths, purely absorbed in the regulation of the life-energy.
- There are still others who curtail their food intake and offer the breath into the life-energy as sacrifice.

Shri Krishna says that all these yogis performing these sacrifices become purified and get rid of their sins.

Those who know the secret of these sacrifices, perform these sacrifices for the pleasure of God. At the end of the offering, they accept the remnants as Prasad or grace of God. Shri Krishna says that partaking of such nectar-like Prasad leads to illumination, purification, and in this way they advance toward the Absolute Truth. Whereas, those who do not perform sacrifices, do not gain anything in this world as well as in the other world and do not become happy.

In this manner, all these different types of sacrifices and religious disciplines are elaborated in the Vedas. All of them originate from the action of body, mind, and senses prompted by the forces of Nature. Understanding this, one gets liberated from the material bondage.

Shri Krishna concludes this topic of different sacrifices by telling Arjun that it is good to perform ritualistic ceremonies, fasts, mantra chants, holy pilgrimages, etc, but if they are not performed with knowledge, they remain mere physical activities. Such mechanical activities are better than not doing anything at all, but they are not sufficient to purify the mind. The cause of bondage is the mind, therefore whatever form of devotion you do, engage your mind in meditating upon God. The discipline of Self-knowledge is superior to any material gain because all actions done with selfless service ultimately resolve into knowledge.

How one can obtain spiritual knowledge (Verse 34 – 42)

The Absolute Truth cannot be understood merely by our own contemplation. The intellect is clouded by ignorance from endless lifetimes and therefore, it cannot overcome its ignorance simply by its own effort. One needs to receive knowledge from a God-realized Saint who knows the Absolute Truth.

Shri Krishna says that to learn the Absolute Truth, you need to approach a spiritual master; Inquire from him with humble reverence and render service to him. Being pleased with you, such an enlightened Saint who has vision of the Truth will impart this knowledge unto you. After achieving enlightenment from a Guru, you shall no longer fall into delusion again. In the light of that knowledge, you will see the entire creation first within your own higher Self, and then within the Lord.

Even if one is the greatest sinner among all sinners, he can easily cross over this ocean of material existence by seating himself in the boat of divine knowledge.

The fire of Self-knowledge reduces all bonds of Karma to ashes, like the blazing fire reduces wood to ashes. Therefore, there is no purifier in this world like the true knowledge of the Supreme Being.

One discovers this knowledge within, naturally, in course of time when one's mind is cleansed of selfishness by Karm Yog. One who has faith in scriptures and words of the spiritual teacher, and one who is committed to gain this knowledge, and has control over the mind and senses, easily gains this knowledge. Having gained this knowledge, one quickly attains absolute peace or liberation.

However, one who has no discrimination, no faith and who is of doubting mind perishes, because for a disbeliever and doubting person, there is no happiness either in this world or next.

Shri Krishna again repeats that actions do not bind a person who has renounced the fruits of actions by Karm Yog and whose confusion and doubts are completely destroyed by the knowledge of the self.

After explaining the importance of Karm Yog and attainment of Self-knowledge, Shri Krishna gives the final call to Arjun to remove your doubts that have arisen in your heart, by piercing with the sword of knowledge and establish yourself in Karm Yog. And thus arise, stand up for the war and do your duties.

- **HARI OM** -

Thus ends the Fourth chapter entitled "GYAN-KARM-SANYAAS YOG"

Do your duty with the attitude of Karm Yoga

- Surrender the fruits of your actions to Ishwar, the Lord.
- Find contentment in the journey you are on, regardless of the outcome
- Whatever we do in the course of our lifetime should be dedicated to the Supreme Being remembering Him in any form - krishna or Rama.
- This will always result in giving us peace and satisfaction and will make us feel God's presence with us all the time, making all our actions turn out to be positive.

Do not expect or fear anything

- Expectations and fears limit our possibilities.
- Accept your desire without any craving to possess it.
- Everyone experiences desires but one should not be moved by them
- Desires should not bother a person, people sometimes undertake really evil actions because of their desires. One should simply not get caught in the chains of desire.

CHAPTER 5 - PATH OF RENUNCIATION

In the first chapter of Gita, it is shown that in the middle of the battle field, Arjun got confused whether he should fight his own people or not and is it worth to kill all of them for some worldly pleasures or even to get Kingdom. He found himself in a no-win situation – if he is victorious, he loses those that are very dear to him, and if he does not gain victory, he is still a loser. He therefore surrendered himself to Shri Krishna to become his disciple and asked him to teach him to find out what is right for him to do.

Shri Krishna starts teaching Arjuna in Chapter 2 from verse 11 onwards. First, He tells Arjun the truth about himself, that you are not this body as such, but your real nature is Atma, which is not subject to death at all. It is neither born nor dies, it is unborn, eternal. In this way, Bhagvaan gives him knowledge about real nature of oneself. He then asks him to do his duty and do his actions and leave the results of actions in the hands of the Lord and thus briefly introduces the Karm Yog and at the end of second chapter, he asks Arjun to be a wise person, who is happy within himself and pursue the path of gaining this wisdom.

After hearing this, Arjun was not sure if he should follow the life style of self Knowledge or the life of actions. Therefore, in Chapter 3, Arjun asked Shri Krishna what is better for him, a life of Karm Yogi or the life of renunciation in pursuit of self knowledge. **Karm Yog** is the chief topic of Chapter 3 and tells Arjun that both these life styles produces the same end result and leads one to same destination of God's abode. However, the life of actions or **Karm Yog is** better since it is easy to follow. He explains to Arjun what **Karm Yog** is. Selfless service, doing all the duties for the welfare of mankind, without expecting anything in return for oneself only is **Karm Yog**. In other words, **Karm Yog** is doing actions with the attitude of renunciation of fruits of actions to the service of the Supreme Lord.

In Chapter 4, Lord Krishna unfolds that **Sanyas** is total renunciation of actions, which is possible only through knowledge. The **Sanyas** means complete renunciation of doer-ship, ownership, and selfish motive behind an action. Complete renunciation comes only after the dawn of Self-knowledge. A Yogi, who gains this self knowledge, sees **"inaction in action"** and **"action in inaction"**. After talking about knowledge in this way, He finally asks Arjun to stand up and fight following the life of **Karm Yog**.

In Arjun mind, this still appeared as a contradiction - if knowledge is the ultimate end gaining which all actions are given up, so why Krishna is asking me to do **Karm Yog** instead of seeking knowledge straight away. Chapter 5 begins with this contradiction in the mind of Arjun and asks Shri Krishna more or less same question which was asked in Chapter 3 also.

Arjun Question in verse 1

Arjun asks, you praise renunciation of all actions; to follow a life style where-in one is free from the obligations of performing all rituals as enjoined by the scriptures and other obligatory duties in this world. On the other hand, you are asking me to follow the life style of **Karm Yog**, asking me to perform my duties. Please tell me definitely which one of these two is better for me.

Description of two life styles (Verse 2- 5)

Lord Krishna said: Both Renunciation and life style of actions without getting attached to fruits of actions, lead to the same supreme goal of liberation. But of these two, the path of performing actions as selfless service (**Karm-Yog**) is superior to the path of complete renunciation of actions (**Karm-Sanyas**) because it is easier to practice for most people.

In this verse 2, Shri Krishna compares Karm sanyās and karm-yog. It has a very deep meaning; so let's understand it in more details.

The Karm Yog is one life style in which a Karm yogi does both, spiritual and social, duties. Social duties are done with the body while the mind is attached to God accepting whatever results come as Prasad of God. On the other hand, Karm sanyās is the life style for elevated souls who renounce social duties due to complete absorption in God, and engage entirely in the performance of devotional service to God. Karm sanyāsīs dedicate their full time and energy to spirituality, while Karm yogis perform both worldly and spiritual duties but with an attitude of complete surrender to God.

At first glance, it looks as though Karm sanyās, doing nothing or doing very little, is easier. But in fact, Karm sanyās is more difficult of the two, if you are not ready for it. Renunciation of all actions means that you should be able to be with yourself, you should be happy with yourself and for that you require certain preparations. That is why, Shri Krishna says, **Karm Yog** is better than Karm sanyās. Karm-yog is thus the safer path for majority of the people, while Karm sanyās is only to be pursued under the expert guidance of a Guru.

Karm yogis continue to discharge their worldly duties while internally practicing detachment. Hence, they neither desire not hate anything and accept both positive and negative outcomes of their actions with equanimity, as the grace of God. Free from attachment and aversions, Karm yogis get easily liberated from bondage of the material world.

Karm sanyās means the renunciation of actions with the cultivation of knowledge. Therefore, one does not become a **Sanyasi** merely by giving up actions and wearing saffron cloths. One has to prepare his mind for the knowledge by following the disciplined life style. A real Sanyasi is one who does not consider himself as owner of what he possesses but he knows that everything belongs to God only. Having given up their sensual pleasures and likes and dislikes, they remain stable and undeterred by difficulties in their pursuit.

Shri Krishna further says that only the ignorant and not the wise, consider the path of Karm Sanyas and the path of Karm Yog as different from each other. The person, who follows even one of these two properly, gets the results of both. The liberation attained by a Karm Sanyasi is also attained by a Karm yogi. Therefore, one who sees the path of renunciation and the path of Karm Yog as identical, they have the true knowledge.

Karm Yog is the preferred life style (verse 6 & 7)

True renunciation or Karm Sanyas (the renunciation of doer-ship and ownership), is difficult to attain without performing the work with the attitude of **Karm Yog**, whereas one who is committed to the life of the **Karm Yog**, quickly attains liberation.

The practice of **Karm Yog** provides the preparation, discipline, and purification of the mind which is necessary to follow the life of renunciation. The Karm yogis whose mind is pure, whose mind and senses are under control, sees God; the soul of all souls; situated in all living beings. Such a person committed to the life of **Karm Yog** does not get affected though engaged in actions and is called Yog yukt (united in consciousness with God).

Characteristics of Yog yukt Karm yogi (Verse 8 & 9)

The Yog yukt is called a wise person and Shri Krishna says that a wise person, who is united in consciousness with God following the life of Karm Yog, thinks himself as non-doer while seeing, hearing, touching, smelling, eating, walking, sleeping, breathing, speaking, giving, taking, as well as opening and closing the eyes. The wise person believes that I am not doing anything; it is only the senses that are operating upon their respective sense objects. They remain situated in the understanding that God is the doer of everything.

Description of a Karm Yogi – Verse 10 - 12

Bhagvaan says that a Karm Yogi does all work as an offering to God, abandoning selfish attachment to results, and therefore, he remains untouched by sins, just as a lotus leaf never gets wetted by water.

As long as our likes and dislikes dictate our activities, we are bound to have problems of irritation, anger and so on. But if you have devotion to the Lord or an awareness of the Lord as Dharma, you are in harmony with the Lord. The **Karm Yogi** performs actions with their body, mind, intellect, and senses without selfish attachment but only for the purification of their mind and intellect.

For the **Karm Yogi**, since the actions are not done for fulfillment of Likes and Dislikes, there is no attachment to the fruits of actions. A Karm yogi does not desire that a given thing should happen or that other thing should not happen. He is happy with whatever happens and hence he gets united with the Lord. While others who perform work to fulfill their desires, get attached to the results of action and remain bound to this world.

Who is a wise person? (Verse 13- 26)

This human body is called a nine gated city, in which the Atma dwells. The nine openings are: Two openings each for the eyes, ears, and nose; and one each for the mouth, anus, and urethra. And who dwells in this body? – The same Atma residing in all beings, which is part of Parmatma Himself.

The wise man who has controlled his mind and intellect and has completely renounced the fruits of all actions, knows that I am not the body but I am the Atma that dwells happily in this body having nine gates. He knows that the Atma residing in this body is neither the doer nor the cause of anything. In other words, a wise man knows that his true identity is the Atma and not the body. It is Atma residing happily in the body which is the witness (sakshi) of all that is happening around.

The Parmatma (Prabhu) neither creates the urge for action nor the feeling of doer-ship nor the attachment to the results of action in people. The body is constituted of the three modes of material nature, and all actions are performed by the three gunas. But out of ignorance, the person identifies himself with the body and becomes implicated as the doer of actions, which are in fact done by material nature. (*In this* ***verse 14****, the word Prabhu has been used for God, to indicate that He is the Lord of the world and controls the entire universe.*)

The omnipresent God is not responsible either for anyone's virtuous deeds or sinful actions. The human beings are deluded because their knowledge about the Self is covered by their veil of ignorance.

But those whose ignorance has been destroyed by the divine knowledge, that knowledge reveals the true nature of the Supreme Entity; just like the Sun illuminates everything removing darkness and reveals the beauty of objects of the world.

Shri Krishna next describes in verse 17 that the enlightened yogi is one whose intellect is fixed in God, whose mind is wholly absorbed in God, who has firm faith in God and considers Him as his supreme goal and sole refuge. Sins of such an enlightened soul are destroyed by the light of knowledge and he quickly reaches the state from which there is no return.

Such a truly learned person perceives God in all living beings, he sees at a learned person, an outcast, even a cow, an elephant, or a dog with an equal vision. Just as a person does not consider parts of the body, such as arms and legs, different from the body itself, similarly a Self-realized person does not consider any living entity different from Bhagvaan but sees one Atma as a tiny fragment of Parmatma, everywhere, in everything, and in every being.

Such a person whose mind is firmly set in equality of vision towards all living beings, conquer this sansaar of repeated births and deaths in this very life itself because there is no rebirth for him. In other words, such a person becomes free from bondage of his actions while living in this world itself and gets liberated from the cycle of birth and death. They become godlike and hence are seated in the Absolute Truth.

The wise person having firm understanding of divine knowledge remains established in God and thus surrenders to the will of the God. They neither rejoice in getting something pleasant nor grieve on experiencing the unpleasant.

Those who do not have any longing for external sensual pleasures; they realize divine bliss within themselves. Being united with the God, such a person gains absolute happiness, the eternal joy within himself that is not dependent upon any thing and which is ever lasting. He becomes one with the Supreme Lord.

Sensual pleasures are, in fact, the source of misery; they give only temporary pleasure to the worldly people. Therefore, the wise person does not revel in them.

One who has been able to withstand the impulses of lust and anger, while living in this world, is a **yogi** and a happy person. One who is happy within himself with a sense of fulfillment, whose mind is illumined by Self knowledge, such a yogi gets united with the God and is liberated from material existence.

Shri Krishna next describes in verse 25, the state of holy persons who are engaged in the welfare of all beings. The sages whose sins have been destroyed and doubts are dispelled by divine knowledge and who are devoted in the welfare of all beings with the disciplined mind, also attain God and gain liberation from material world.

Karm Sanyas also leads to same goal (verse 26 – 29)

Thus far in this chapter, Shri Krishna has extolled the path of karm-yog. He now speaks in the remaining four verses for the Karm Sanyasi, revealing that they too attain the final goal.

Shri Krishna states that true Karm sanyāsī who have eliminated the urges of desire and anger through constant effort, who have subdued their mind, and are self-realized also make rapid progress and experience perfect peace both in this life and here-after i.e. they gain Moksh.

Shri Krishna then describes the dhyan yogi who practices meditation on the name and form of God. Such yogis shut out thoughts of sense enjoyment by focusing their mind in the middle of their eyebrows and equalizing the flow of the incoming and outgoing breath in the nostrils in

a rhythmic action. This yogic process enables them to control their senses, mind, and intellect. In this way by practice of meditation and always concentrating on the ultimate goal, that sage become free from lust, anger, and fear, and thus also gains liberation.

In this way, the devotee having united his soul with the God, realize that the God is the enjoyer of all sacrifices and austerities; He is the supreme Lord of all the worlds and the selfless friend of all living beings. Such a devotee attains peace by grace of God. This is the final state of Brahma gyan (God Realization).

- **HARI OM -**

Thus ends the Fifth chapter entitled "KARM SANYAS YOG"

Atma, the soul is our true nature

Our true nature is not this body but the Atma, which is immortal, pure and sat-chit-anand. It is not subject to destruction by any means and when this body is gone, it takes birth in another form or body. The person who knows this truth is never really troubled by sadness or grief.

CHAPTER 6 - MEDITATION

In last three verses of chapter 5, Krishna had introduced the topic of Meditation, which is the topic of teaching in chapter 6. All human beings in this world have likes and dislikes which generate desires. In fulfilling these desires, we do actions and follow whatever means that are necessary to accomplish the chosen end. We don't care if our actions are right or wrong, but attached to our desires; we choose any means required to get that desire fulfilled. Such persons are activist. On the other hand, the approach of a Karm yogi is different, often implying some renunciation on his part, the main criteria of doing actions being conformity to Dharma and Adharma. A Karm yogi renounces his likes and dislikes and does whatever needs to be done but without being guided by his likes and dislikes or results of actions and therefore, is also a kind of a Sanyasi.

The Karm yogi is not a complete Sanyasi but has the quality of a Sanyasi in terms of renunciation of his likes and dislikes. Sanyasi is one who gives up scriptural activities as well as worldly activities , and all other activities born out of likes and dislikes, in terms of worship, family duties, business, to be more clear, he has no more roles to play as son, daughter, parent, friend etc.

Thus, in order to gain freedom from this world of bondage, one has to do Sadhna, and this Sadhna is twofold - external and internal. Karm Yog is the external means which is for purification of the mind by freeing oneself from one's Rag-Dvesh. The internal means is Mediation, which is for steadiness of the mind. Both, external and internal means are meant to prepare the mind for knowledge to gain Liberation, and freedom from birth and death.

Arjun was confused and did not know what path he should follow for self realization - the path of Renunciation or the path of Karma. In Chapter 5, Lord Krishna explained to Arjun that both these paths are in fact same and both lead to the same ultimate destination. No one can remain without doing any action in this world; even a person who has renounced the world and become a Sanyasi also performs actions naturally to sustain life. He further explains that the path of Karm Yog is easy to follow and practice than the path of renunciation and therefore asked Arjun to be a Karm yogi and perform his duties.

In first two shloka of chapter 6, Bhagvaan talks about Karm Yog and Karm Sanyas Yog, which were also discussed in previous chapters as a means of gaining liberation.

First two verses in Chapter 6

Lord Krishna begins by telling Arjun that one, who performs the prescribed duty without seeking its fruit for personal enjoyment, is both a Sanyasi and a Karm Yogi. One does not become a **Sanyasi** merely by not lighting the fire, or merely by abstaining from work. Shri Krishna says that **Sanyas** is same as Karm Yog and no one becomes a Karm Yogi who has not renounced his attachment to the fruit of action or who has not relinquished the selfish motive behind an action. Karm Yog is a means to become a true Sanyasi.

Path to attain perfection in Yoga (Verses 3 – 4)

In chapter 3, verse 3, Shri Krishna had mentioned that there are two paths for attaining liberation—the path of renunciation and the path of action. Between these two, he recommended to Arjun to follow the path of action. Again in chapter 5, verse 2; he declared Karm Yog to be the better path. Does this mean that we must keep doing Karm Yog all our life?

Anticipating such a question, Shri Krishna says in verse 3 of chapter 6, that for those who are aspiring for perfection in Yog, the path of Karm Yog is the means and therefore more suitable. But for the elevated souls who has no desires for sensual pleasures and whose mind has been purified by following the life style of Karm Yog, the path of Meditation is more suitable. (*In this verse, Shri Krishna has used the word 'Yog-ārukṣhu' for those sādhaks who aspire for union with God and have just begun climbing the ladder. For them the path of Karm Yog is the recommended means. The word 'Yog-ārūḍha' has been used for those who have become elevated in their pursuit of union with God after following a life of Karm Yog and they practice Meditation with their mind fixed upon God.)*

When one performs action as a matter of duty without any selfish motive, has no desires to fulfill and is free from fear of failure and thus his mind has become tranquil, that person is said to be elevated in the science of Yog and becomes ready for yogic perfection through meditation.

Importance of controlling the mind (verse 5 – 7)

Tranquility of mind is very important, Bhagvaan says, because the mind alone is one's friend as well as one's enemy. The mind is the friend of those who have control over it, and the mind acts like an enemy for those who do not control it. There is no bigger enemy other than an uncontrolled mind in this world.

Vedic scriptures tell us that lust, anger, greed, envy, illusion, etc. which reside in our own mind are the biggest enemies. These internal enemies are even more damaging than the outer ones. The external demons may injure us for some time, but the demons sitting within our own mind have the ability to make us live in constant wretchedness. When we nourish hatred in our mind, our negative thoughts do more damage to us than the object of our hatred. Therefore, an uncontrolled mind is one's enemy.

However, the same mind has the potential of becoming our best friend, if we bring it under control of the intellect, through spiritual practice. A controlled mind can accomplish many beneficial endeavors, whereas an uncontrolled mind can degrade the consciousness with most ignoble thoughts.

Shri Krishna says that we must use our intellect (Buddhi) to control the mind. The yogis, who have conquered the mind, rise above the dualities of cold and heat, joy and sorrow, honor and dishonor. Only those yogis remain peaceful and steadfast in their devotion to God, who have controlled their mind and senses from worldly enjoyments and selfish desires. **The sovereign recipe to cleanse the mind from the defects of lust, anger, greed, envy, and illusion, is to detach it from the world and attach it to the Supreme Lord.** Therefore, one should first try to control and conquer this enemy by following the path of Karm Yog and then do regular practice of meditation with a firm determination and effort.

Spiritual Practice of Meditation for Conquest of Mind – verse 7

Meditation is effortless control of the natural tendency of the mind to wander and tuning it with the Supreme. The mind becomes the cause of bondage when controlled by sense objects and the same mind after being controlled by the intellect, becomes the cause of liberation, and gets attached to the Supreme. Therefore, after establishing control over the activities of the mind, one should take the mind away from the enjoyment of sensual pleasures and fix it on God. In this way, the sense impulses become ineffective because the senses obtain their power from the mind. One who becomes master of the mind becomes master of all the five senses. When mind becomes under control, he remains unaffected in heat and cold, in pleasure and pain, in honor and dishonor, and remains ever steadfast with the Supreme Being. Just as the reflection of the moon in a lake can only be seen when the water is still, similarly, the Parmatma can only be realized when the mind becomes still.

Description of a Yogi – verses 8 & 9

In these two verses, Shri Krishna describes who can be called a yogi.

Bhagvaan Krishna has used the phrase **'gyan-vigyan-triptatma'** for a yogi first. Gyan is the theoretical understanding obtained by listening to the Guru and from the study of the scriptures, whereas Vigyan is the realization of that knowledge as an internal awakening and wisdom from within and triptatma means fully satisfied through gyan and vigyan. Therefore, a person is called yogi who is fully satisfied about the Supreme Lord through both knowledge and Self-realization.

Then Shri Krishna says – a yogi is **'kuṭastha'** which means that the yogi neither seeks pleasurable situations nor avoids unpleasurable ones and thus his mind is always composed in every situation.

A yogi is **'Vijitendriya'**; he has subjugated the senses by having control over his mind. He thus remains a **Yog-yukt**; in constant communion with the Supreme Lord. For such a yogi, a clod, a stone, and gold are the same since the material energy belongs to God only.

Endowed with realized knowledge of God, the yogis see the whole creation in its unity with God. Thus, they see all human beings whether they are well-wishers, friends, foes, acquaintances, mediators, relatives, the saints, or the sinners with equality of vision. Such a yogi with equal vision towards all beings is the most exalted Yogi. This is the highest level of state of Yog when the yogi sees the entire universe, with all its living and non-living beings as the manifestation of the Supreme Being, who dwells within it.

This state can be achieved by meditation (Verses 10 to 19)

Having stated the characteristics of one who has attained the state of Yog, Shri Krishna now talks about how it can be achieved.

A yogi who has been able to keep the mind and senses under control and who has become free from desires and proprietorship should reside in secluded and quiet place alone and constantly engage in contemplation upon the Supreme Lord.

To practice the Meditation, the yogi should sit in a clean place on a firm seat that is neither too high nor too low, covered with grass, a deerskin, and a cloth, one over the other.

Sitting there in a comfortable position and concentrating the mind on God, controlling the thoughts and the activities of the senses, one should practice meditation to purify the mind and senses. One should sit by holding the waist, spine, chest, neck, and head erect, motionless and steady and fix the eyes and the mind steadily on the front of the nose without looking around.

In this way, with a serene, fearless, and unwavering mind, and firmly established in the commitment of Brahmcharya (practice of celibacy), the vigilant Yogi should meditate on Parmatma as his supreme goal. The definition of celibacy is not restricted to mere abstinence from physical indulgence but also from mental thoughts of any such nature.

In verse 15, Shri Krishna then gives the ultimate benefits of meditation.

A yogi of disciplined mind, keeping the mind constantly absorbed in God in this way, attains *'nirvan'* (liberation from material bondage) and thus abides in Supreme Abode in peace.

Shri Krishna next defines some regulations which need to be followed while doing Meditation.

The success in this Yog is not possible for those who eat too much or who do not eat at all, who sleep too much or too little. A healthy mind and body are required for successful performance of any spiritual practice. Therefore, it is required that a yogi should regulate his daily bodily functions, such as eating, sleeping, bathing, resting and recreation. Those who eat too much or too little may become sick or fragile. It is recommended to fill half of the stomach with food, one fourth with water, and leave the rest empty for air. If one sleeps more than six hours, one's lethargy, passion, and bile may increase. A yogi should avoid extreme indulgence in uncontrolled desires as well as too much control by torturing of the body and mind.

With thorough discipline, they learn to withdraw the mind from selfish cravings and focus the mind exclusively on God. Such a person with disciplined mind automatically becomes free from all desires and is said to have achieved Yog i.e. union with the God.

In verse 19, Shree Krishna gives the simile of the flame of a lamp. When there is wind, the flame flickers naturally and is impossible to control; however, when there is no wind, the flame becomes steady. Similarly, the mind is fickle by nature and very difficult to control. But when the mind of a yogi is disciplined by the practice of meditation, it becomes steady and sheltered against the wind of desires. In this way, the Yogi feels infinite bliss by the practice of Meditation and abides in the Self.

Results of Yog Sadhna (verse 20 to 23)

After presenting the process of meditation and the state of its perfection, Shree Krishna now reveals the results of such Sadhna.

When the mind is purified, one is able to perceive the Self as distinct from the body, mind, and intellect. For example, if there is muddy water in a glass, we cannot see through it. However, if we put alum in the water, the mud settles down and the water becomes clear. Similarly, when the mind is unclean, it obscures perception of the soul and any acquired scriptural knowledge of the Atma is only at the theoretical level. But when the mind becomes pure, the soul is directly perceived through realization.

After realizing the Absolute Reality, one is never separated from it. In this joyous state of Yog, one experiences supreme boundless divine bliss. It stems from the fact that we are tiny fragments of God, who is an ocean of Bliss.

Having reached that state, for a Yogi, there is no other gain as better than that and he is not moved even by the greatest calamity. For example, every person strives hard to become rich, but when he becomes millionaire, he starts thinking of becoming a billionaire, and thus discontentment sets in again. No matter what happiness we get, the feeling of unfulfillment lingers on. Shri Krishna says that happiness achieved from the state of Yoga is the infinite bliss of God and there is no more to be gained by him.

In verse 23, Shri Krishna says that Yoga is the state of dissociation from association with misery. Thus when a person attains divine supreme bliss, all his miseries come to an end. This Yog should be resolutely practiced with determination free from pessimism.

How to practice Meditation? (Verse 24 - 28)

Meditation requires the dual process of diverting the mind from the world and fixing it on God. Shri Krishna begins by describing the first part of the process - taking the mind away from the world by renouncing all desires that arise in the mind. One should first restrain the senses from running towards the sense objects with the mind. Through gradual and repeated exercise and with conviction in the intellect, the mind will become fixed in God alone and thus will not think of anything else.

Shri Krishna further says that the path to perfection in Yog is long and arduous since mind is very frickle. It will wander off in the direction of infatuation inspite of our best efforts. However, when it does wander off, one should again take the mind away from the sense objects and bring it back to God. By repeated practice of this, the mind's attachment toward God will start increasing and simultaneously, its detachment from the world will also increase. As this happens, it will become easier and easier to meditate.

As a yogi who thus perfects the practice of withdrawing the mind from sense objects and fixing it upon God, his passions get subdued; the mind becomes utterly serene and he becomes sinless. Such a Yogi attains great transcendental happiness and he sees everything in connection with God. Shri Krishna explains that the self-controlled yogi thus uniting the Self with Brahman becomes free from all sins and achieves the highest state of perfect happiness.

Oneness between Jeeva and Lord (verse 29 – 32)

In these verses, Shri Krishna explains equality among all human beings and Parmatma.

- A yogi, who is in union with the Parmatma, sees every one with an equal eye everywhere and sees the Atma abiding in all beings and all beings abiding in the Supreme Being. Shri Krishna says that those who perceive me in everything, and behold everything in me, are not separated from me, and I am not separated from them.
- A Self-realized person sees Me in the entire universe and in oneself and sees the entire

universe and oneself in Me. When one sees Me pervading everything, just as fire pervades wood, he is at once freed from delusion, though engaged in all sorts of activities.

- The best yogi is one who regards every human being like oneself and who can feel the pain and pleasures of others as one's own. The wise see their own higher Self present in the entire universe and the entire universe present in their own higher Self.

Arjun Question - Controlling mind is very difficult (verse 33 - 34)

Listening to all this about doing the meditation while controlling the mind, Arjun responded by saying that this system of Yoga or Meditation appears to me impractical and difficult to be endured since the mind is restless and unsteady and can wander here and there in matter of fraction of seconds. Arjun says that he finds mind to be more difficult to control than the wind.

What Arjun said is absolutely true - we are living in a materialistic world wherein our mind is subject to continuous agitation. We are always thinking and trying to change our situation with a hope that we can get rid of our mental agitation at some point. But it is the very nature of this materialistic world that we cannot be free from anxiety and we remain in a dilemma at all the time. So if a person of the qualification of Arjun, who was a great warrior and whom Lord Krishna chose to be his disciple, finds it immensely difficult , then for common persons like us, it may be even impossible.

Krishna's reply - Mind can be controlled by spiritual practice of meditation:

Lord Krishna replied that undoubtedly, the mind is restless and difficult to restrain, but it can be controlled by Vairāgya and practice. The first step is to control the mind by detachment from worldly objects which eradicates the unnecessary wanderings of the mind. Then the next step is to practice this by concerted and persistent efforts and bring the mind to fix on the Lord i.e. by Meditation.

Shri Krishna further says that Yog is difficult to gain for one who has not mastered his mind. However, those who have brought the mind under their control through persistent efforts can achieve success by adopting the proper means.

Arjun Question (Verses 37 – 39)

This created a doubt in Arjun's mind regarding the sādhak who is unable to control the mind and therefore asked Shri Krishna – "What is the destination of a Yogi who had full devotion but he deviated from the path of meditation and failed to attain yogic perfection since he was not able to keep his mind under control at the last moment?. Does he get deprived of both worldly and heavenly pleasures and perish like a dispersing cloud?"

A cloud, which breaks away from the group of clouds, becomes worthless. It neither offers sufficient shade, nor does it increase its weight and become rain-bearing. It merely blows in the wind and perishes like a non-entity in the sky. Giving this example of a perishing cloud, Arjun asks whether the unsuccessful yogi suffers a similar fate, with no position and without any support in this world and heaven. Arjun pleads with Shri Krishna to completely dispel this doubt because he knew that it is only the God who can dispel such a doubt.

Arjun's question is very pertinent, because the mind is very difficult to control and therefore, it may not be possible to achieve perfection during one's lifetime. Does all the effort get wasted?

Spiritual Practice of a Yogi never goes waste (Verses 40 – 47):

Lord Krishna says that there is no destruction for a person who engages on spiritual path, neither here in this life nor in the later life. A seeker, who strives for God, never reaches a bad end.

In this chapter, Yog has been used in the context of 'Union with God'. Such a person, who has not been able to succeed in their spiritual path, goes to celestial abode called higher worlds like heaven. After living there for countless years, he is again given birth on this earth in the family of pious and prosperous one's.

Residence in the celestial abodes is awarded to those who engage in mundane virtuous deeds and the fruitive Karm-kāṇḍ activities enjoined in the Vedas. They are unsuccessful in Yog (Union with God) because of their desire for enjoying the sensual pleasures was not overcome. So such a fallen yogi is sometimes sent to the celestial abodes for a long time, and then again granted birth on earth either in the house of a pious family that will nurture the spirituality in him from childhood, or in the house of a wealthy family where all the bodily needs are taken care of and one does not need to engage in the struggle for survival. Such a family environment facilitates the opportunity to engage in spiritual pursuits for the souls who are so inclined.

God has an account of all our thoughts and actions of endless lifetimes. In accordance with the law of karma, the spiritual assets (Puny) earned by the unsuccessful yogi in the previous life bear fruits. Accordingly, such a person, who had traversed quite a distance and developed dispassion, is not sent to the celestial abodes. But he is born in the family of spiritually advanced parents to facilitate the continuance of his spiritual journey. Such a birth is a great fortune because the parents inculcate divine wisdom in the child from the very beginning. Just as a traveler may break his journey to rest in the night in a hotel and on waking up he simply moves ahead to cover the remaining distance; likewise, by God's grace, the yogi of past lives receives the previous spiritual assets accumulated, and continues the journey from where he had left off as if has woken up from sleep.

There, he regains the knowledge acquired in the previous life and strives again to further success in Yog and achieve perfection. He is instinctively carried towards God by virtue of the impressions of yogic practices of previous lives. Such seekers naturally rise above the ritualistic principles of the scriptures. Such a Yogi strives even harder than before and gets cleaned of all the impurities of the mind, and ultimately becomes completely free from all sorts of material desires. In this way, he attains perfection in Yog in this life itself and reaches the Supreme Abode after death.

Shri Krishna says in verse 45 that "Perfection in Yog is the result of the accumulated practice of many lives."

Yogi is most superior to all (verse 46 & 47)

A yogi is superior to the tapasvī (who lives an extremely austere life style); he is superior to the Gyani (a person engaged in cultivation of Knowledge), and even superior to the Karmic person (who performs the Vedic rituals for attaining material opulence and the celestial abodes). Shri Krishna declares the yogi to be superior to them all because the yogi strives not for the world, but for God while the goal of all others is worldly attainment. As a result, the yogi's accomplishment is at the spiritual platform and is superior to them all.

In last verse of this chapter, Shri Krishna declares that even amongst all yogis, I consider them to be the highest whose mind is always absorbed in Me, and who engage in devotion to Me with great faith. In this verse, Shri Krishna has used the word 'bhajate'. It comes from the root word bhaj, which means "to serve." It is a far more significant word for devotion than "worship," which means "to adore." Here Shri Krishna says that the one, who not merely adores Him, but also serve Him with loving devotion, is the most superior among all Yogis.

- **HARI OM -**

Thus ends the Sixth chapter entitled "DHYAN YOG"

In verse 9, Shri Krishna has described different types of people in this world and a person is a Yogi who is impartial towards all of these and has no love or hatred towards any of these….

- **Suhird** is one who extends a helping hand without expecting anything in return.
- **Mitr** means a friendly person with whom you share a certain understanding or friendship
- **Ari or Shatru** means enemy, who is inimical towards you
- **Udaseen,** with whom you just have an acquaintance of saying hello, like the person whom you meet at a bus stop some time or the other. In case of a fight between two such people, he remains neutral and joins neither side.
- **Mediator,** one who arbitrates and solves the problems or rift between two friends, he is interested in both of them and whatever he decides, will be acceptable to both of them.
- **Dveshi**, one who deserves to be disliked by you because of his actions
- **Bandhu**, your own relatives whose opinion really affect you. Because you want them to have a good opinion of you, they can control you emotionally and psychologically.
- **Sadhu** –person who follows very closely what is enjoined by the Dharma, follows what is right and avoids what is wrong.

- **Paapi** – Opposite of Saadhu is a Paapi, he does actions what is not to be done and what is to be done is not done.

What is Perfect Happiness or Divine Bliss?

In this chapter, Shri Krishna has used the word Divine Bliss which means Perfect Happiness.

In Spiritual terms, Happiness can be classified into four categories:

i) *Tamasic* happiness which is derived from drugs, alcohol, cigarettes, meat products, violence, sleep, etc.

ii) *Rajasic* happiness which is derived from the gratification of the five senses and the mind.

iii) *Sattvic* happiness which is the pleasure experienced through practicing virtues, such as compassion, service to others, cultivation of knowledge, stilling of the mind, etc. It includes the bliss of self-realization experienced by the Gyanis when they stabilize the mind upon the Brahman.

iv) *Nirguna happiness*. This is the divine bliss of God, which is infinite in extent.

CHAPTER 7 – GYAN VIGYAN YOG

In first six chapters, Shri Krishna has talked about the meaning of the word Tvam, 'you' the Jeeva or the individual soul in the mahavakya "TAT TVAM ASI". Now in the following six chapters, the word Tat, the cause of everything, the Lord, is the predominant topic. Chapter 7 thus starts with the description of Ishvar, the Lord and his real nature.

In verses 1 – 3 of seventh chapter, Bhagvaan starts by telling Arjun that he can know Me, the Lord of all beings, fully without any doubt, with the mind absorbed in Me, surrendering to Me, and performing yogic practices. Shri Krishna says that this knowledge which I am going to tell you is an immediate knowledge, which is a reality that I see and not just based on hearsay, after knowing which nothing more remains to be known in this world. This knowledge is very rare because only one in thousands makes an effort to gain it and it is difficult to gain also because only one in thousands of those seekers, truly understands it.

THE CAUSE OF CREATION (verses 4 – 7)

Shri Krishna now starts the description of Bhagvaan from 4th verse of this chapter. Lord Krishna first reveals two fold cause of creation (Two Prakriti). Shri Krishna tells that

- One is my svabhav or apara Prakriti, which is the immediate cause of this creation, consisting of the five elements – earth, water, fire, air, and space along with mind, intellect and ego. This eightfold material Nature is called lower energy or material energy. It creates the material world.
- The other Prakriti is my svarupa Prakriti, or para Prakriti or Chetan Prakriti, My higher Nature, which is the cause of everything, by which the whole universe is sustained. This higher Nature is called higher energy or the spiritual energy. This is also called consciousness, the soul.

The Supreme soul known as Parmatma is the efficient cause of creation of the universe.

The Apara Prakriti and the Para Prakriti are not two independent identities but these are two aspects of the Supreme Lord. The Atma, and material Nature are the same yet different as the Sun and its light and heat are the same as well as different.

All creatures, living or non living in this world, everything known and unknown, have evolved from this twofold Prakriti, two fold energy, and the supreme soul is the source from whom everything comes as well as into which everything dissolves. There is no other cause which is superior to the Supreme Being. Everything in the universe is woven into the Supreme Being, like cluster of beads are strung together on the thread of a necklace.

Modern science tells us that matter is a combination of 118 elements discovered so far. However, in the Vedic philosophy and the Bhagavad Gita, matter is considered as part of God's energy and called Prakriti. It is further divided into eight forms, as listed in this chapter.

Albert Einstein was the first to come out with the theory of Mass-Energy Equivalence in 1905. He proved that it is possible to convert mass into energy and numerically presented it by an equation $E=mc^2$. His Theory of Relativity replaced an earlier concept of the universe made of solid matter. Both these theories were challenged in 1920 by Niels Bohr and other scientists with Quantum Theory, which proposes a dual particle-wave nature of matter.

More than 5000 years ago, long before the development of modern science, Lord Krishna had disclosed the perfect Unified Field Theory. He said to Arjun, "All that exists in the universe has manifested from My material energy." The material energy has extended itself into infinite shapes, forms, and entities of this world.

PARMATMA IS IN EVERY THING

In next four verses (8-11 verses); Shri Krishna shows how each and every thing is non-separate from Me, the Parmatma.

Lord says, I am the taste in the water, I am the light in the Sun and the Moon, I am "OM" in all the Vedas, the sound in the space and strength in human beings. (*It is the intrinsic property of water to carry the taste of all substances; without water, there will be no taste. In the same way, Akaash (space) acts as the vehicle for sound. Different languages form due to sound modifications. Shri Krishna says He is the origin of it all, as the taste in water and sound in space is His energy.*)

Shri Krishna further says that on Earth, He is the force behind both the non-living and the living. He is the sweet fragrance of the earth and the bright radiance of a flame. He is the life-force of all living creatures. He is the force behind the spiritual discipline in ascetics.

Bhagvaan is the cause (eternal seed) from which all beings manifest. He is the subtle force behind the intelligent and the glorious. He only makes their minds more analytic and thoughts scintillating.

He is the serene and sublime strength in people, which empowers them; to successfully fulfill their duties and responsibilities and also devoid of passion and attachment.

Lord says - I am the Desire that is according to Dharma, meaning that I am that very form of desire due to which this creation exists. Suppose a person has a lot of talents, skill and wisdom, but no desire to do anything, then it all just remains inside. Therefore, Bhagvaan says any desire which is in keeping with the Dharma, in keeping with the universal order is because of Me.

Anything beautiful in this universe has come out of such a desire.

In verse 12, Shri Krishna sums up all his glories what He described in previous four verses. He says that all material objects, good, bad or ugly are made possible only by My energy, I am the essence of everything. He further says that even though the entire creation originates from God, He is beyond His creation and independent of it.

Maya, the divine power of God (verse 13 - 15)

The omniscience Lord Krishna was aware that the following question will come to Arjun's mind, "If such are your Vibhutis (opulence), then why most humans forget that you are the Supreme creator and controller of this entire creation?" Therefore, He clears this doubt from Arjun's mind by himself. He says that the people in this world are unable to know me as essence of everything due to the delusion caused by the three modes of His Maya (the material energy) that are ignorance, passion and goodness. The word "Maya" is made from mā (not) and yā (what is). Thus, Maya means "that which is not what it appears to be" and due to this Maya of the Lord, people get deluded.

It is very difficult to overcome this divine power called Maya of Bhagvaan. In second line of verse 14, Shri Krishna says, "Only those can smoothly cross this Maya, who surrender themselves to Me, the Supreme Lord." In next verse, Lord Krishna says that there are four categories of people who do not surrender to Me and hence they cannot cross this Maya, the ocean of material existence.

i) The Ignorant who lack spiritual knowledge and thus indulge in wrong actions.
ii) The lazy who have the knowledge and awareness of what they need to do but still due to their lazy-nature do not want to surrender to the Lord.
iii) People with deluded Intellects who are so proud of their intellect that they have no faith in the scriptures and the teachings of the saints.
iv) People of devil Nature who do not like God and His glories and dissuade others also from surrendering to the Lord.

DEVOTEES OF GOD (Verse 16 – 19)

Shri Krishna now describes four types of virtuous people who worship or seek the Supreme Lord:

- The seeker of wealth, who worship with a desire to gain wealth,
- The distressed, who worship to get rid of some danger to them,
- The seeker of Self-knowledge, who has desire for devotional love of God
- And the enlightened devotee or Gyani Bhakt who has experienced the Supreme Being.

Bhagvaan says that among them the enlightened devotee, who is ever united with Me and whose devotion is single-minded, is the highest because I am very dear to him and he is very dear to Me.

In the next verse 18, Shri Krishna clarifies that all these seekers are indeed noble and blessed souls, but the Gyani Bhakt is my own Self because with his steadfast mind in Me, he has become one with Me and abides in My Supreme Abode.

Shri Krishna says that it is only after many births of spiritual practice of seeking true knowledge, one gets enlightenment and God realization. It is only then, he surrenders to Me. Such a great soul is indeed very rare.

Worship of Devtas (celestial gods); verses 20 - 24

From verse 20, Shri Krishna starts explaining what happens to those who do not follow the path of knowledge but their mind is carried away by material desires and worship devtas for fulfillment of their desires which arise in their mind due to their very own nature. Depending upon their desires, they perform particular type of worship; for example if one wants a son, he performs prescribed ritual meant for the birth of a son. Material desires shroud their knowledge and hence, they forget that the Supreme Lord is the source of all that exists, including these celestial gods.

These people do not know that all these celestial gods also occupy different positions in the working of God's creation. They derive their powers from God; they are not independent of Him. They can bestow on their devotees only material things that are under their control. But cannot liberate anyone from the bondage of Maya or the cycle of birth and death because; they themselves are not liberated from this cycle. God alone has the power to do so; God alone is eternal; all others are perishable including celestial gods.

Bhagvaan says that anybody who worships whichever devta with faith, I make their faith firm in that very form. If they worship that devta with firm faith, they gain their desired objects or wishes through that devta, but those wishes in fact have been granted by the Supreme Lord only. However, such material gains of these human beings of limited knowledge are temporary. People who worship the devatās go to the planets of the respective devatās upon death. Whereas, those who are devoted to Me, come to My abode."

The ignorant person does not understand the limitless, changeless nature of the Supreme Being who has no form and beyond which there is nothing greater. They consider Me as a human being having particular form going through birth and death like others. Shri Krishna further says that by virtue of my divine power (Maya), I do not reveal myself to such an ignorant person who do not know and understand Me as one who is unborn, eternal, changeless and formless.

True Nature (Swarup) of Bhagvaan; verse 25 - 26

Shri Krishna had mentioned two of His divine energies earlier in this chapter, in verses 7.4 and 7.5- The eightfold Prakriti, or the material energy, and the jīva Shakti, or the soul energy. Now, He talks about His third and the most powerful energy that is the Yogmaya. God descends in this world by virtue of His Yogmaya energy. However, the same Yogmaya power keeps His divinity concealed from us and we are unable to feel His presence, although He is seated in our hearts.

Therefore, Shri Krishna says to Arjuna that "I know all beings of the past, of the present, and those of the future, but no one with finite talent really knows Me". God is all-knowing and omniscient, but He is beyond the scope of our intellectual logic.

Delusion caused by pairs of opposites (Dualities); verses 27- 30

Having given a glimpse of His omniscience in the previous verse, Shri Krishna now tells Arjun that all beings in this world are in utter ignorance due to the delusion of pairs of opposites arising from desires and aversions; likes and dislikes; happiness and pleasures, heat and cold; birth and death and so on.

But the persons of pious deeds due to which his sins have been washed off, becomes free from the illusion of dualities and worships God with firm resolve.

Only those persons who surrender to the Supreme Lord completely, take shelter in Him and thus strive for freedom from the cycles of birth, old age, and death; come to know of the true nature of Supreme Self, the Brahman. Such true devotees, who remember God even at the time of death, attain His divine abode. Those who understand God to be the governing principle of the whole creation, the underlying basis of all Temporal Beings, the sustainer of all entities, and the enjoyer of all sacrifices and pleasures, attain Liberation.

- **HARI OM -**

Thus ends the Seventh chapter entitled "GYAN VIGYAN YOG"

CHAPTER 8 – AKSHAR-BRAHM, THE IMPERISHABLE BRAHMAN YOG

In last two verses of Chapter 7, Lord Krishna talks about a wise man who at the end of their life time, leaves this material body remembering the true nature of the God and reaches me without any doubt. In doing so, He introduces several new words. Arjuna did not fully understand the meaning of these new words and also he could not quite understand how a wise person should keep his mind steady in real nature of God at the time of his death. This becomes the basis for the questions which are formulated by Arjun in first two verses of Chapter 8. Shri Krishna while explaining the meaning of these words, further elaborates and explains to Arjun how a wise person can attain Moksh and can become free from the cycle of birth and death.

Arjun asks seven questions in first two verses:

1. What is that *Brahman (Absolute Reality)* which you say the wise men know;

2. What is *Adhyatam (Individual soul)*, which you say is centered in the Self;

3. What is the meaning of *Karma* here;

4. Who is that *Adhibhutam*, that is centered in all the beings;

5. What is *Adhidevam* who is said to be centered on all the gods?

6. Who is *Adhiyagya* in this body and

7. How people with a steady mind, can remember you and keep you in their mind at the time of death.

Shri Krishna answers the first six questions in next two verses:

- **Brahman** is the Supreme Being who is limitless and not subject to any change whatsoever. The creative power of Supreme Being is the cause of creation of the whole world. In Vedas, God is referred to by many names and Brahman is one of them.
- The Soul, the subtle body or Atma that resides in every physical body in the form of awareness is **Adhyatam.** The subtle body keeps the physical body active and alive by operating the organs of perception and action.
- **Karma** here means actions or rituals in which there are offerings which is the cause of birth of human beings.
- All physical bodies i.e. all manifestations of the five elements—earth, water, fire, air, space that exist in

this world and are constantly changing, are called **Adhibhutam**.
- **Adhideva** is the universal form of God, which presides over the celestial gods in this creation and encompasses the entire material creation.
- **Adhiyagya** is the Supreme Divine Personality, who dwells in the heart of all living beings as the *Paramātmā* (Supreme Soul), who sustains everything in the Universe.

The last seventh question of how to remember Parmatma at the time of death is answered in next 4 verses (5 – 8).

Krishna says that one, who always remembers the Supreme Being, even while leaving the body at the time of death, will certainly attain the Supreme Abode. Therefore, one should always remember God, the Supreme Being, keeping his mind and intellect centered on Him and only then he will remember the Lord at the end of the life, because one remembers only that object at the end of life, which he has been always thinking of and seeking for throughout his life.

Shri Krishna says – The Supreme abode can be attained by constantly remembering God, meditating upon Him and always keeping his mind resolved in Him.

To meditate upon 8 Attributes of Supreme Lord (verse 9-10)

Shri Krishna then describes 8 divine attributes of God upon which one should meditate:

- God is all knowing, one who sees every thing - past, present and future;
- God is eternal, non-destructible and without any beginning and end;
- He rules the whole creation, because of whom the law of Dharma and all other laws exist in the creation;
- He is sustainer of all, just as the ocean is the supporter of waves;
- He is subtler than the subtle; He is even subtle than the soul;
- He is formless but exists every where and cannot be seen;
- He illumines the whole world as Sun ;
- He is beyond the darkness of ignorance. Just as the sun can never be covered by the clouds, even though it may seem to us that it has been obscured, similarly God can never be covered by the material energy Maya even though He may be in contact with it in the world.

Bhakti of Bhagvaan (verse 10 – 13)

From verses ten to thirteen, Shri Krishna describes how one should contemplate upon Bhagvaan with an unwavering mind disciplined by the practice of meditation.

When one leaves the physical body by controlling all the sense organs, focusing the mind upon God and engaged in yogic practice of holding the breath in the middle of his forehead, between the eye brows, and steadily remembering the Lord with full devotion, certainly attains Supreme Abode.

Scholars of Vedas describe Parmatma as '*Akshara*' meaning imperishable; great saints practice the vow of celibacy and renounce all worldly pleasure to attain Him.

Lord Krishna now tells briefly the method of contemplation

Krishna says, one should first restrain all the gates of the body from their normal outgoing tendencies; fixing the mind upon God in one's heart region, and then one should draw the life- breath towards the head. In this way, one should remain in Yogic concentration. One who departs from the body while remembering the Lord, and chanting the syllable Om, will certainly attain the supreme goal.

This is extremely difficult and requires a lifetime of practice. In verse 14, Shri Krishna gives an easy way of gaining such mastery.

"I am easily attainable by that devotee who exclusively always thinks of Me; and whose mind does not go elsewhere." Here Shri Krishna emphasizes upon Bhakti Yog; which is worship of God in any of His Human Form with unwavering mind. Such a person is called here as Nitya Yukta - One who is endowed with a mind that is always tranquil, whose mind is always under control and remains steadfast upon Bhagvaan only.

After attaining the Supreme Abode, such great souls do not gain another birth, which is cause of sorrow and misery, because they have attained the state of highest perfection. In verse 16, Shri Krishna says that everyone 'in all the worlds' of this material creation, up to the highest abode of Brahma, is subject to rebirth. But there is no further rebirth for the Yogi who attains the Supreme Abode of Parmatma.

Let's first find out what is meaning of 'all the worlds' mentioned by Shri Krishna in this verse. The Vedic scriptures 5000 years ago has described that there are fourteen worlds in our universe - Seven planes of existence lower than the Earth called Narak - tal, atal, vital, sutal, talātal, rasātal, pātāl; and seven above including Earth (bhūh). The ones above the earth are called Swarg or celestial abodes namely bhuvah, swah, mahah, janah, tapah, satyah. The highest amongst them is the abode of Brahma, called Brahm Lok or satyah Lok. (In contrast, as late as in the sixteenth century, Nicholas Copernicus was the first western scientist to propose a proper heliocentric theory stating that the Sun was in fact the center of the universe. Until then, the entire Western world believed that the earth was the center of the universe. Subsequent advancement in astronomy revealed that the Sun was also not the center of the universe, but revolving around the epicenter of a galaxy called the Milky Way. Further progress enabled scientists to conclude that there are many galaxies like the Milky Way, each of them having innumerable stars, like our Sun.)

Therefore, Lord Krishna says in this verse that all of these fourteen lokas are within the realm of Maya, and hence subject to the cycle of birth and death. These have been referred in the previous verse as *duḥkhālayam* and *aśhāśhvatam* (impermanent and full of misery).

However, those who attain God-realization, they cross even the Brahm Lok and attain the divine abode of Parmatma; get released from the bondage of the material energy and thus do not have to take birth in this material world again.

Vedic scriptures also describe that some saints do come back even after liberation from Maya; but they do so only to help others get out of bondage as well. These are the great descended Masters and great Prophets, who engage in the divine welfare of humankind.

Description of Brahm lok and its time period

Now Shri Krishna tells Arjun that this creation is subject to time and not eternal. Therefore, know from Me the time period of this cycle of creation and destruction.

(The Vedas state that one day and night of the celestial gods, such as Indra and Varun, corresponds to one year on the earth plane. Thus one year of the celestial gods, consisting of 30 × 12 days is equal to 360 years on the earth plane.

Vedas also state that 12,000 years of the celestial gods correspond to one mahā yug (cycle of four yugas) on the earth plane; which means 4.32 million years on earth plane. This can also be calculated as given below:

Each mahā **Yuga** consists of four stages – satyug, Tretayug, Dwaparyug and Kalyug. The time period of each of these four stages is as follows:

- **Kalyug** lasts for 432,000 years
- **Dwapar yug** lasts twice of **Kalyug** meaning 864,000 years
- **Treta Yug** lasts three times of **Kalyug** meaning 1,298,000 years
- **Sat yug** lasts four times of **Kalyug** meaning 1,728,000 years

Thus total duration of one mahā yug (the sum total of above four stages of Yug) is 4.32 million years of solar system.

Brahma's one day lasts one thousand mahā yugas or 4.32 billion years, which is called kalp and is the largest unit of time in the world. Brahma's one night also lasts one thousand mahā yugas. Brahma creates the planetary systems and their life forms when he wakes up and dismantles them before *sleeping. Brahma ji lives for 100 years as per Vedas; meaning 36000 years of solar system.)*

Shri Krishna thus describes the time period of this cycle of creation. He says that when Brahmaji day breaks, all the manifest individuals, Sun, moon, stars, planets, inert and sensitive entities come into existence as Brahmaji wakes up from his sleep. Just as from our sleep, our day starts when we can experience the world, similarly Brahma ji wakes up from his sleep, the whole creation comes about in existence.

When Brahmas night comes (*after 4.32 billion years*), all things that were manifest, dissolve or go back to the cause, Brahma ji *(for 4.32 billion years)*; this is called pralaya or partial dissolution. Exactly like our own world resolves into us in sleep night after night and comes back again day after day, in a similar way, the whole creation resolves during Brahma's day and dissolves at Brahma's night.

(One cycle of evolution and dissolution thus goes on for 8.64 billion years. At the end of Brahma's life of 100 years, the entire universe including the Brahm Lok is dissolved. Thus this cycle of creation goes on for almost 311 trillion and 40 billion human years. This is called mahapralay or great dissolution.)

In Verses 20 & 21, Shri Krishna says that there is yet another eternal existence beyond this manifest and unmanifest creation, which does not perish when all created beings perish. This eternal realm is the supreme goal attaining which one never returns to this mortal world. This supreme goal is also called the Supreme Abode of the God.

In verse 23, *Shri Krishna declares that the God; the Parmatma, can be attained only through Bhakti.* The Supreme Lord exists everywhere, He is all pervading, all living beings are situated in Him and He is also present in every atom of the material world. He can be reached only by unwavering devotion to the Supreme Lord.

In Bhagvad Gita, Shri Krishna has repeatedly emphasized upon the need for Bhakti to know God and attain Him. In this verse, He explicitly adds the term 'ananyayā', which means "by no other path" can one know God. One may practice ashtanga yoga, engage in austerities, accumulate knowledge, and develop detachment. Yet, without devotion, one will never attain God.

Now Shri Krishna describes **in verses 23 -26; two different paths** departing which during death, the yogis either do not return to this world or come back to this world.

The Path of Light

The six months of the Sun northern course, the bright fortnight of the moon and the bright part of the day which are all characterized by light, is called the path of light. Light is symbolic for knowledge. Those, whose consciousness is established in God and detached from sensual pursuits and depart by the path of light, they attain the Supreme Abode of God, and are released from the wheel of sansaar.

Path of darkness

Six months of the Sun southern course, the dark fortnight of the moon and the night which are all characterized by darkness, is called the path of darkness. Darkness is symbolic for ignorance. Those who practice Vedic rituals governed by their desire for materialistic world and depart by the path of darkness, go to heaven, the celestial abode. After enjoying celestial pleasures, and when the fruits of their virtuous deeds are exhausted, they again return to the earth.

These two, bright and dark paths, always exist in this world. The path of light leads to liberation and the path of darkness leads to rebirth. The path of light represents the life style of spiritual practice and Self-knowledge while the path of darkness represents materialism and ignorance. The former leads to Liberation and the latter leads to rebirth as human beings.

Yogis who know the secret of these two paths, are never bewildered and do not get distracted at all. Therefore, they always remain situated in Yog; in Union with God. The yogis, knowing this secret, gain merit far beyond the fruits of Vedic rituals, the study of the Vedas, performance of sacrifices, austerities, and charities and attain the Supreme Abode.

- HARI OM –

Thus ends the Eighth chapter entitled "AKSHAR BRAHM YOG"

CHAPTER 9 – THE KING OF MOST SECRET KNOWLEDGE

In the two previous chapters, Shri Krishna declared that among all Yogas, Devotion to the Lord or Bhakti is the highest and simplest path of attaining Yog, or union with the Supreme. In Chapter 9, Shri Krishna explains that there is only one God, who is the sole object of worship and the final goal to reach for all human beings. Therefore, those souls who engage in exclusive devotion towards the Supreme Lord go to His abode and remain there. Those influenced by the ritualistic ceremonies described in the Vedas also attain the celestial abodes. However, when their merits are exhausted, they must return to earth.

Krishna first reveals about the true knowledge which one needs to gain and that knowledge is to understand very well that the whole world - Sun, Moon, stars, known and unknown - is not separate from the Self. Parmatma is everything, He is limitless and infinite.

This knowledge alone is the direct means for liberation, nothing else and not meditation, Karmas, attitude or values, though all of them are indirectly helpful to gain a mind that can grasp this knowledge. Like fuel, vessels and so on are all needed for cooking, but all of them together can not cook. For that you require Fire. Similarly for liberation, the direct means is the knowledge - I am Brahman, nothing else. However, to gain this knowledge, preparedness is what accounts for whether this knowledge takes place or not. 1+1=2 is impossible for an infant to understand because he is not yet prepared. For knowledge that I am Brahman to take place, the mind preparedness is a certain maturity or assimilation of the experiences of life, which is must. This knowledge is like the Einstein formula E=mc2, you can write it thousand times but still you can not understand it till your mind is prepared to get this understood. In chapter 9 and subsequent three chapters, Shri Krishna declares that mind can be prepared to gain this knowledge only through pure Bhakti or true devotion to the Supreme Lord.

In first two verses of Chapter 9, Shri Krishna says to Arjun that He is going to impart this secret knowledge to you whom He found was fully prepared to gain that knowledge and knowing which you will be released from the miseries of material existence. Lord Krishna calls this knowledge as greatest secret since even though it has been taught many times before, but it has not been understood very well and that is why it remained as secret inspite of being revealed many times in Scriptures.

Shri Krishna declares that this knowledge is the king among all knowledge (raj-Vidya) and **most secret** of all. It is supreme secret not because it is not known, but because it is too sacred and pure. The divine love for the supreme Lord is too sacred because it purifies and liberates the devotee from insecurity, fear, sorrow and limitations and purifies him from these worldly objects. It is directly perceptible, virtuous and very easy to practice.

Again the question arises, where this knowledge is kept hidden that it becomes the most secret of all. Our Spiritual books say that this knowledge is hidden within yourself and that is why it remains secret until you discover it within yourself.

This knowledge is also most secret because it is not something that can be gained by any known means like perception, or by our experience. Perception, evidence or understanding can be by two ways - by sense organs and witness perception. Seeing the printed word in a book is a perception through sense organs while the conditions of your mind like happy and sad are known to you as a witness, or proof. Since the knowledge of Brahman is not a perception of either of the two above means and nor is going to be an experience, therefore there is no way of knowing "I am Brahman" unless you have another evidence or proof.

Because it is not available for any known proof, it is the most secret. From another stand point, this knowledge is most secret since it is very precious and rare. If you are in possession of a large diamond, which is very rare and precious, you will keep it secret from the general public for the fear of being stolen.

Now the question arises, what I will gain from this knowledge "I am Brahman"? Suppose I tell you a secret that crows have no teeth, what you get out of it? When I say you are Brahman, you can say "if I am Brahman, let it be so, what difference does it make to me?" Krishna says that I am not just going to tell you that you are Brahman but going to prove it. That is why this knowledge is scientific and knowing this that you are Brahman, you will get immediate release from sorrow, from the inadequacy, the smallness and the bondage of the Self from this world.

This knowledge is called the **king** among all disciplines of knowledge. This knowledge is called the King among all the knowledge because having gained this knowledge, there is nothing else to be gained, it is complete knowledge. For example, when a person completes his PhD degree, he knows how much he had to study, but still how little he has understood. His every sentence could be a research material for another Ph.D. This goes on and on so that no one is satisfied with his knowledge even in a given field, leave alone so many other disciplines of knowledge.

This knowledge of the Self, called Atma-Gyan is the greatest purifier - knowing which your ego is gone and when ego is gone, you become the non doer of any karma. It not only cleanses of all karmas done in this life, but it eliminates all your Punya and Papas in previous lives also.

This knowledge is "directly perceptible"; by practice of the science of Bhakti with unflinching faith which results in direct perception of God and this is very easy to practice also. It is not unlike the methodology of other sciences, where we begin an experiment with a hypothesis and conclude with a verified result.

Krishna says in **verse 3**, that those who do not have faith in God, they remain in this world of death and birth. In order to have direct perception of God, it is must to have firm belief and faith in God and follow the spiritual path to gain the Self Knowledge.

There is a beautiful story regarding perception of God. A king once asked a Sadhu, "I do not believe in God because I cannot see Him. Can you show me where He is?" The Sadhu asked for a cow to be brought to king's court. The cow was brought and the Sadhu then requested that it be milked. The king instructed his servants to milk the cow. The Sadhu asked, "O King! Do you believe that this milk, freshly taken out from the cow, contains butter?" The king said he had full faith that it did. The Sadhu said, "You cannot see the butter in the milk. Then why do you believe it is there?" The king replied, "We cannot see it at present because the butter is pervading the milk, but there is a process for seeing it. If we convert the milk into yogurt, and then churn the yogurt, the butter will become visible." The Sadhu said, "Like the butter in the milk, God is everywhere in the whole universe. We cannot directly see Him, for that there is a process of Bhakti and spiritual path to be followed like churning of milk to see the butter in it."

Shri Krishna now explains this Secret Knowledge; verse 4 - 6

Shri Krishna says, "This entire cosmic manifestation is pervaded by Me in My unmanifest (**Niraakaar**) form. All living beings dwell in Me but I do not dwell in them." *Thus Lord Krishna conveys the Vedic concept that here is one God; He is seated in everyone's heart; He is also everywhere in the world. God pervades everything that has existed and all that will exist.*

In next verse Shri Krishna says, "And yet no living beings abide in Me due to my mysterious divine energy called Yogmaya. Although I am the Creator and Sustainer of all living beings, yet I am not influenced by them or by material nature."

In these two verses, Shri Krishna has said that though I abide in all living beings, yet no living being abide in Me. Apparently, this statement seems contradictory, therefore, let's understand it with some examples.

Like in every gold chain, there is Gold but Gold is not a gold chain. Gold chain exists because of gold but gold does not exist because of gold chain, which is only given a form and name. Similarly, waves depend on the ocean but the ocean does not depend on the waves. But if you look more deeply, there is no wave or ocean, it is water only. Now the wave is water, but the water is not wave. Water is present in the air as vapours, in clouds, rain, ice, as well as in the bubble, the lake, the river, the wave, and the ocean. These are nothing but names of different forms (or transformations) of water. When one understands this very well, for him there is no ocean, no wave, and no lake, but water only. However, a wave is a wave as long as it does not realize its true nature – that it is not a wave but water. When the wave realizes that it is water, the wave no longer remains a wave, but becomes water.

Similarly, when one realizes that he is not this physical body but the Eternal Being in the form of Atma residing inside the physical body, one immediately becomes one with the Parmatma without undergoing any physical change. As a physical body, one is mortal, limited by a form, with color, gender, and temperament. But as a part of the **Parmatma**, one is free, immortal, and limitless.

This is also explained by Lord Krishna in verse 6 by giving the example of the wind. Just as, the mighty winds that blow everywhere yet always remains within the sky (space), in a similar way; all living beings dwell within God. However, God remains ever aloof and detached from all these activities as a neutral observer by His divine Yogmaya power.

Cycle of Creation (verse 7 to 10)

Shri Krishna explained in the last two verses that all living beings dwell in God. In that case, the question may come in our mind that where do all the living beings go when mahapralay comes? In the previous chapter, verses 8.16 to 8.19, Shri Krishna had explained how the creation, maintenance, and annihilation follow a repetitive cycle during the life span of 100 years of Brahma ji. In verses 7 & 8 of chapter 9, Shri Krishna explains what happens to living beings at the end of one *'kalp'*; the end of Brahma ji life span.

Shri Krishna explains that at the end of one *'kalp'*, all living beings merge into My Prakriti, the primordial form of material energy and goes into an unmanifest state into the divine body of the Supreme Lord. Their gross and subtle bodies merge back into the source, Maya. However, the causal body still remains. At the beginning of the next creation, I manifest them again. In accordance with their causal bodies, they again receive subtle and gross bodies, and the various life forms are created in the universe. I create the entire multitude of various forms again and again according to their Karmas with the help of My Prakriti and keep them under control of the modes of my Prakriti.

Bhagvaan further says that these acts of creation do not bind Me, because I remain like a neutral observer and unattached to those acts. It is only My divine kinetic energy called Maya, working under my direction that creates all animate and inanimate forms and thus the creation keeps on going.

Deluded persons do not recognize Shri Krishna as God incarnation (verse 11 & 12)

Shri Krishna says that the ignorant people do not recognize Me and consider Me as a common human being in this world. Due to delusion, they cannot see divinity in Me as the Supreme Lord of all beings and do not consider Me as incarnation of God. Such ignorant people having Tamsic qualities and who remain attached to their materialistic desires, embrace devil means. In that deluded state, all their hopes for welfare are in vain, their cryptical (or secretive) actions are wasted and they remain confused.

Wise people worship God in many ways (verse 13 – 15)

However, the great souls having Satvic qualities know My true nature as material and efficient cause of this universe and worship Me with devotion keeping their minds focused on Me alone. They do kirtan and sing my divine glories with loving devotion with great determination and humbly bowing down to me.

While those, who engage in the spiritual path to gain true knowledge, worship Me by many methods. Some see Me as one Supreme Being non-different from them while others worship My various forms separate from them. There are still others, who worship Me in the infinite manifestations of My cosmic form.

Glimpse of infinite personality of God; verse 16-19

In verses 16 & 17, Shri Krishna first reveals a glimpse of His divine personality. He says that "I am the Vedic rituals, I am the Yagya meaning sacrifice, I am the oblation that is offered to ancestors, I am the medicinal herbs, I am the chants of mantras, I am the ghee offered as oblation, I am the ritual fire and any act of offering to God."

He further elaborates that "I am the father of the world (I am the creator the world), I am also the mother (who holds the unmanifested material energy into the womb), I maintain the universe and nourishes it (Sustainer) and I am the Grandfather of this universe too."

"I am that what is to be known (True Knowledge), I am that which purifies, I am the sacred syllable Om, and the one to be known by Ṛig Veda, Sāma Veda, and the Yajur Veda."

Then, in verse 18, Shri Krishna says that "I am the Supreme Goal of all living beings, and I am also their Sustainer, Master, Witness, Abode, Shelter, and Friend. I am the origin, end and resting place of creation. I am the one from whom the whole creation has come and into whom everything is resolved and in whom everything has its existence."

He further elaborates in verse 19 that; "I energize, light up and radiate heat as the Sun, I withhold and release rains. I am immortal and I am also death. I am the cause and effect of this Universe."

In these verses, Shri Krishna has explained the nature of the Supreme Lord and His divine glories briefly and His relationship with the world. In Summary - Each individual Atma is a tiny part of God and therefore our every relationship is with God only. However, in bodily consciousness, we look upon the relatives of the body as our father, mother, beloved, child, and friend. We become attached to them and repeatedly bring them to our mind, thereby getting further bound in the material illusion. But none of these worldly relatives can give us the perfect love that our soul yearns for. All these relationships are temporary, and separation is unavoidable. Our relationship with them is based on our selfishness and so it fluctuates in direct proportion to the extent by which self-interest is satisfied. Thus, the range and intensity of worldly love with them varies from moment to moment. On the other hand, God is such a relative who has accompanied us lifetime after lifetime. From birth to birth, in every life-form that we went, God accompanied us and remained seated in our heart. He is thus our eternal relative. In addition, He has no self-interest from us; He is perfect and complete in Himself. He loves us selflessly, for He only desires our eternal welfare. Thus, God alone is our perfect relative, who is both eternal and selfless.

Our relationship with God is like the relationship between ocean and wave that emerge from it. Two neighboring waves in the ocean flow together for some time, and play mirthfully with each other, creating the impression that they have a very deep relationship between them. However, after travelling some distance, one subsides into the ocean, and shortly after, the other does the same. Thus both the waves were born from the ocean and their relationship was with the ocean itself. Similarly, God is like the ocean and we are like waves who have emanated from Him. We create attachments amongst our bodily relations, only to leave everyone upon death, and journey alone into another birth. The truth is that the souls, the Jeevatma are not related to each other, but to God, from whom they have all emanated. From the platform of the soul, God alone is all our relationships; He is our Father, Mother, Sister, Brother, Beloved, and Friend.

Different levels of worship; verses 20 - 22

Shri Krishna then reveals different levels of worship, the highest level of worship being the devotion and worship of the Supreme Brahman.

Those who perform Vaidik rituals to specific gods like Indra (the rain god), Sun, Kuber (the god of wealth), Agni (the god of fire), etc., go to that plane of experience known as Heaven and live there till they exhaust the results of their good actions. Celestial delights of the heavenly abodes are temporary. After they have fully enjoyed heavenly pleasures and exhausted their merits, they are sent back to the earthly plane. In other words, they remain in this cycle of birth and death and therefore are subject to miseries and do not get liberated by performing Karam Kand (Vedic rituals).

Then there are those who always remember God with exclusive devotion and surrender to the Supreme Divine, Param Brahm and Parmeshvar, the cause of every thing. Shri Krishna says that I provide them what they lack and preserve what they already possess.

Shri Krishna finally concludes in verses 23 and 24 that even those devotees who faithfully worship other gods also worship Me, though they do not know that these gods also receive their powers from Me only. By virtue of the powers bestowed upon them by the Supreme Lord, they do possess the ability to grant material favors, but they cannot liberate their devotees from the cycle of life and death and therefore they are reborn.

Such people do not know that when they worship devtas, they worship Me only, but due to ignorance, they do not recognize Me as the real recipient of their worship. They worship different gods for fulfillment of their various desires and to enjoy various luxuries etc. Because of that, they limit themselves to that particular experience.

In verse 25, Shri Krishna explains the implications of worshipping different entities by revealing the varieties of destinations attained. Those who worship celestial gods, they go to their abode. Those who perform various rituals for ancestors like shradh etc. go to their world called Pitrilok after death. Pitr are the departed souls living in a particular plane of experience which is more desirable than this world, called Pitrilok. Then there are tthose who out of their ignorance worship sprits and ghosts like Yaksh, Rakshas; take birth amongst them.

However, the highest devotees who firmly resolve to worship God and engage steadfastly in His devotion go to His divine Abode after birth.

Once you recognize that the Lord is every thing, the result will be limitless. There is no coming back because the ego is gone, you get librated. Not only that, inspite of result being so great, it is achieved easily once you attain that knowledge, because it is already a fact about you. For sugar to be sweet, what should it do? It simply has to know - "I am sweet" Similarly, I am limitless - is simply a thing to be known.

Shri Krishna further says that to please Me and gain My grace, it is not necessary to perform complicated rituals, but only with love and devotion and dedicated heart, whosoever offers Me a leaf, a flower, a fruit, or water with devotion, I accept that offering with love.

In fact , whatever one does by body, mind, senses, thought, intellect, action, and speech, should be done with the thought that it is all for God only and in this way, you shall become free from the bondage of your good and bad Karmas and attain supreme abode by this attitude of complete dedication to God.

Shri Krishna says that all living beings are equal to me; I am neither inimical nor partial to anyone and I have a uniform law of karma according to which I bestow My grace. Any devotee who worship Me with love, reside in Me and I reside in them.

As an example; the rainwater falls equally upon the earth. Yet, the drop that falls on the cornfields gets converted into grain; the drop that falls on the desert bush gets converted into a thorn; the drop that falls in the gutter becomes dirty water; and the drop that falls in the oyster becomes a pearl. The raindrops cannot be held responsible for this variation in results, which are a consequence of the nature of the recipient. Similarly, God states here that He is equally disposed toward all living beings, and they get benefit of His grace according to his nature and Karmas.

Shri Krishna says that even the most sinful person, once he resolves to worship Me with single-minded, loving devotion, is regarded as a righteous person because he has made the right choice and resolution, and soon he becomes righteous and attains everlasting peace. Lord Krishna declares that a devotee never fails to reach God. Irrespective of their birth, sex, caste, or race, whoever takes complete shelter of God, will attain the supreme goal. What then to speak about kings and sages with meritorious deeds? Such is the greatness of the path of devotion that everyone is eligible for it.

Therefore, having obtained this joyless and transitory human life, one should always worship God with loving devotion. This human body is very difficult to obtain, this is the jewel of creation and it is only in human life, one can achieve higher levels of existence and can become free from bondage of birth and death. All other forms of life on the earth, except human life, are devoid of higher intellect and discrimination.

Having said so, Shri Krishna concludes this chapter by asking Arjun to always think of Me, be devoted to Me, worship Me, and bow down to Me. Thus, uniting yourself with Me, by setting Me as the supreme goal and the sole refuge, you shall certainly come to Me.

- HARI OM -

Thus ends the Ninth chapter entitled "RAJ VIDYA RAJ GUHMYAMTAM YOG"

CHAPTER 10 - THE GLORIES OF BHAGVAAN

In tenth chapter of Gita, called **Vibhuti Yog**, Lord Krishna presents the glories of the **Parmeshvar**. Even though God is all pervasive and is everything, still the glories of God are seen in certain places and in some persons from time to time. In fact, in whichever situation, whichever object there is glory or beauty, it is to be recognized as attributed to God and needs to be appreciated.

In first 11 verses of this chapter, Lord Krishna tells his glories briefly to Arjun, knowing which the devotees of God come out of the darkness of ignorance. In next 7 verses, Arjun requests Shri Krishna to explain to him his divine glories in detail. In rest of this chapter, Bhagvaan tells his glories in details.

In Verse 22, Bhagvaan says "I am the mind among all sense organs". In fact all the organs are from Him only but Mind is most important since all senses have the mind as their basis, without which none of the others can function. It is through the mind that we gain the knowledge of the world and through mind only we order our sense organs to perform their respective function. Mind thus receives data from all sense organs. Mind is thus the glory of the Lord, the **Parmeshvar**.

In this shloka itself, God says I am Intellect in all living beings; Intellect means the faculty of cognition, the capacity to understand and inquire, thus gaining clarity of knowledge (maturity) as well as free will.

Chapter 10 begins with Shri Krishna telling Arjun that listen from me my glories briefly, which even celestial gods and sages do not know my origin because I am the source from which all the celestial gods and seers come.

Bhagvaan says that those who know Him as unborn and beginning less, and as the Supreme Lord of the universe, they among mortals are free from illusion and become free from all evils.

In verse 4 & 5, Shri Krishna mentions twenty emotions that manifest in a variety of degrees and combinations in different people to form the individual fabric of human moods, temperaments, and dispositions, all of which emanate from Him. These are:

- Buddhi - ability to analyze things in their proper perspective,
- Gyanam - knowledge to discriminate spiritual from material,
- Asammoham - Freedom from Confusion,
- Kshma- forgiveness,
- Satyam - truthfulness,
- Dama - restraining the senses from the sense objects
- Shama - mastery over the Mind,
- Sukham - emotion of joy and delight,
- Duḥkham - emotion of sorrow and affliction,
- Perception of existence
- Perceptio of destruction,

- Fear of oncoming difficulties,
- Fearlessness,
- Ahinsā - abstinence from harming any being through word, deed, or thought,
- Samatā - equanimity in good and bad situations,
- Tuṣhṭi - feeling of satisfaction in whatever comes by ones karma,
- Tapa - religious discipline,
- Dān - giving charity to one who is worthy,
- Yash- fame in possessing good qualities,
- Ayaśh or ill-fame for possessing bad qualities

And many more such qualities manifest in living beings to the extent sanctioned by Him alone.

In verse 6, Shri Krishna mentions twenty-five elevated personalities that are born of Him. These are the seven Rishis, the four great Saints, and the fourteen Manus. From them, all the people in the world have descended.

There is no doubt that those who know this truth about My glories and divine powers, they naturally become unwavering devotee of God and become united with Him through Bhakti Yog.

God is the Supreme Ultimate Truth and the cause of all causes. He is the origin of whole creation and because of Him everything is sustained.

Those who have exclusive love and devotion in God, whose mind is always focused in Him, surrendering their lives to Him, they derive pleasures in conversing about glories of God and mutually enlightening each other. Out of compassion for them, God who dwells within their hearts, destroy the darkness born of ignorance, with the luminous lamp of knowledge.

ARJUN PRAISES SHRI KRISHNA; Verse 12 - 18

Hearing all this, Arjun was completely convinced about the supreme position of Shri Krishna and reveals his understanding of what he has learnt so far and said to Shri Krishna;

"You are limitless Brahman, light of all lights, you are the Creator and Lord of all beings, source of all the gods, the Supreme person, and Lord of the universe. All the saints and sages, including Narada, have told in this manner and you yourself have also told me. All this vision which you have told me, I consider it as true indeed. Neither the gods nor the Rakshas know your absolute reality. You alone know yourself by yourself. Therefore, you alone are able to fully describe your own divine glories or the manifestations by which you exist pervading all the universes. Please explain to me again, in detail, your yogic power and glory; because I am not satiated by hearing your nectar-like words.

Lord Krishna then explains to Arjun His prominent divine manifestations only because there is no end to a detailed description of the Lord.

God is the ātmā of the ātmā (Soul of the soul) of all living beings; Verses 20 – 39; In these verses, Krishna has described 82 of his infinite opulence.

Lord Krishna says "God is enthroned in the heart of all living beings. He is the beginning, middle, and end of all living beings. The whole creation has emanated from Him, and so He is their beginning. All life that exists in creation is sustained by His energy, and so He is the middle. And those who attain liberation go to His divine abode to live eternally with him. Hence, God is also the end of all living beings."

Amongst the twelve sons of Aditi, He is *Vaman* who was the Avatar of Lord Vishnu; amongst luminous objects He is the Sun; His *vibhūti* (opulence) manifests in the wind called "Marichi; He is the moon among the stars.

Amongst four Vedas, God is the Sāma Veda which describes God's glories as they manifest in the celestial gods, who are incharge of administering the universe; He is Indra amongst the celestial gods who is chief among them.

God is the mind among the senses because all senses function due to the presence of mind. Consciousness exists in all living beings by the divine power of God; therefore Shri Krishna says "God is the sentience in the sentient."

Among eleven Rudras, God is in the form of Lord Shiva as Shankar. Among Yakṣhas (semi-divine demons) God is their leader, Kuber who is the god of wealth and the treasurer of the celestial gods. Amongst eight Vasus, God represents Agni that gives energy to rest of the elements and He is Meru among the mountains (Meru is a mountain in the celestial abodes famed for its rich natural resources and therefore it reveal the vibhūtis of God).

Among the priest, He is Brihspati; among warriors, He is Kartikeya, the son of Lord Shiv; and ocean among the reservoirs of water.

Among the great sages, God's glory is revealed best in Bhrigu. God among His formless aspect is "AUM"; He is Gayatri mantra among the spiritual disciplines; and Himalaya among the mountains which best displays His opulence.

His glories are also seen in the holy Peepal tree (sacred fig tree) among the trees; in Narada among the sages; in Chitrarath among the Gandharvas; and in sage Kapil among Sidhas.

Amongst horses His glories are in Ucchaihshrava horse begotten from the churning of the ocean of nectar; in Airavata amongst all lordly elephants, and in the king amongst humans.

Know Him as the Vajra (thunderbolt) amongst weapons; Kamadhenu amongst the cows; Kaamdev, the god of love amongst all causes for procreation; and Vasuki amongst serpents.

Know Him as Anant among divine serpents, on whom Lord Vishnu rests; as Varuna who is celestial god of Oceans; as Aryama among ancestors, the third son of Aditi; as Yamraj, the celestial god of death who dispenses justice on behalf of God.

Know Him as Prahlad amongst the demons; as Time amongst all that controls birth and death; as the lion amongst animals; and Garud amongst the birds.

Know Him as the wind among the purifiers; Lord Rama among the warriors; the crocodile among the water creatures and the holy Ganges River among the rivers.

God is the beginning, middle, and end of all creation; the science of spirituality amongst sciences which liberates the human being from material bondage and Vada the logical conclusion in all debates.

Know Him to be the first vowel of alphabet "A" amongst all letters (In Sanskrit, all letters are formed by combining a half-letter with "a."); know Him dwandva compound among all dual words; He is the endless Time, and Brahma amongst creators.

God devours everything in the form of death. In the cycle of life and death, those who die are born again. Shri Krishna states that he is also the generating principle of all future beings. The virtues of fame, prosperity, perfect speech, memory, intelligence, courage, and forgiveness that make women glorious are from God. All these qualities are His Vibhuti.

Amongst the hymns in the Sāma Veda His glories are most prominent in the Brihatsama. The poetry of the Vedas is in many meters. Amongst these, the Gayatri meter is very attractive and melodious and Gayatri mantra is set on this. Shri Krishna says amongst poetic meters I am the Gayatri. Of the twelve months of the Hindu calendar, Shri Krishna says He is the months of Margsheersh, and of seasons He is spring season which brings forth flowers.

In verse 36, Lord Krishna says, "I am the gambling of the cheats." Question may come to our mind that how gambling is the glory of God? The answer is that God has given the freedom of choice to human beings. This is just as electric power can be used both to heat and cool a house; the user is free to choose how to utilize the power. However, the powerhouse that supplies the energy is not responsible for either the use or misuse of the power. Similarly, a gambler too possesses intellect and ability that is supplied by God. But if he decides to misuse these God-given gifts, then God is not responsible for the sinful deeds.

God's glories are also present in splendor of the splendid, in victory of the victorious, in resolution of the resolute, and in goodness of the good. In fact, all virtues, achievements, glory, victory, and firm resolve originate from God.

Shri Krishna further says "amongst the descendants of Vrishni, I am Krishna, amongst the Pandvas I am Arjun, amongst the sages I am Ved Vyas and Shukracharya amongst the great thinkers."

Proper punishment to prevent lawlessness, the path of righteousness followed to win victory, silence among secrets and wisdom of the wise; all signify powers of God.

In verse 39, Shri Krishna again states that God is the generating seed of all living beings, no creature moving or non-moving can exist without Him. Living beings are born in four ways: Aṇḍaj—born from eggs, such as birds, snakes, and lizards; Jarāyuj—born from the womb, such as humans, cows, dogs, and cats; Swedaj—born from sweat, such as lice, ticks, etc; Udbhij—sprouting from the earth, such as trees, creepers, grass, and corn. There are also other life forms, such as ghosts, evil spirits, manes, etc. God is the origin of all of them and the power of rulers, the statesmanship of the seekers of victory.

Conclusion

In verse 40, 41 and 42, Lord Krishna concludes this chapter by saying, "there is no end to my divine manifestations. I have declared only a mere sample of my infinite glories. Whatever beautiful, glorious, or powerful is seen in this world, it springs from just a spark of my splendor."

Having revealed many amazing aspects of His splendor, He says that the magnitude of His glory cannot be judged even from the sum total of what He has described. He pervades and supports this entire creation just within a fraction of His divine power.

- **HARI OM** -

Thus ends the Tenth chapter entitled "VIBHUTI YOG"

CHAPTER 11 - Yoga of the vision of the cosmic form

After telling his glories briefly in the tenth chapter, in last verse Bhagvaan Krishna had said that I pervade this entire universe with only one small fraction of myself. Arjun was wondering if it is really so? He had also heard about what happened when Yasoda asked Krishna to open his mouth upon finding him eating the mud and then when child Krishna opened his mouth, she saw the entire world within the little mouth of Krishna. Therefore, a curiosity developed in the mind of Arjun to see that entire cosmic form within the form of Krishna who is standing in front of him. And what is that cosmic form – the single form which includes all forms is called the cosmic form. In this cosmic form, Arjun saw wheel of time destroying everybody. He saw continuous dissolution and evolution of the universe within the cosmic form, seeing which he got frightened. This is the sum and substance of the Eleventh Chapter.

In first four verses, Arjun requests Lord Krishna with prayers that my illusion is dispelled by the profound words of wisdom you have narrated to me about the origin and dissolution of beings and your glory and I totally believe in what you have said, yet I wish to see your divine cosmic form, O Supreme Being.

After listening to Arjun's prayers, in verses 5 – 8, Shri Krishna asks him to have a vision of his viśhwarūp, or universal multifarious divine form with infinite shapes and colors in which you can see all the celestial beings and the entire creation; animate and inanimate, all at one place in my body. But you are not able to see me with your physical eyes; therefore, I give you the divine eye to see my majestic power and glory. Having said this, Lord Krishna, revealed His supreme majestic form to Arjun.

In verses 9 to 14, Sanjay narrates to king Dhritrashtra the description of what Arjun saw in the cosmic form of Lord Krishna. Sanjay says that Arjun saw the Universal Form of the Lord with many mouths and eyes, divine weapons and ornaments, with faces on all sides, illumined like thousands of Suns in the sky and entire universe standing all in one body of Krishna.

Seeing all this, Arjun was filled with wonder; and with his hairs standing on end, bowed his head to the Lord and prayed with folded hands.

Arjun describes the Cosmic Form (verse 15 to 31)

Arjun then describes what he has seen and says to Lord Krishna that I behold in your body all the celestial gods and hosts of different beings. I can see Brahma seated on the lotus flower; I see Shiv, all the sages, and the celestial serpents. I see you everywhere with infinite forms, with many arms, stomachs, faces, and eyes without beginning nor the middle nor the end. I see you as omnipresent, all pervading, shining all around like the immeasurable brilliance and blazing fire of the Sun.

You are the Supreme imperishable Being, You are the ultimate resort of the universe, You are the Soul and protector of the eternal order (Dharma). I see you with infinite power pervading the entire space between heaven and earth in all directions. Your power has no limits. Your arms are infinite; the sun and the moon are like your eyes, and fire is like your mouth. I see you warming the entire creation by your radiance. Seeing your marvelous and terrible form, the three worlds are trembling with fear.

All the celestial gods are taking your shelter by entering into you. In wonder, some are praising you with folded hands; the great sages and perfected beings are admiring you with auspicious hymns and profuse prayers. The Rudras, Adityas, Vasus, Sadhyas, Vishvadevas, Ashwini Kumars, Maruts, ancestors, Gandharvas, Yakshas, Asuras, and Siddhas are all beholding you in wonder.

Seeing your infinite form with many mouths, eyes, arms, thighs, feet, stomachs, and many fearful tusks, the worlds are trembling with fear, and so do I. Seeing your form touching the sky, effulgent in many colors, with mouths wide open and enormous blazing eyes, my heart is trembling with fear. I have lost all courage and peace of mind. I lose my sense of direction and find no comfort after seeing your mouths with fearful tusks glowing like fires of cosmic dissolution. Have mercy on me, O Lord of celestial rulers, and refuge of the universe!

I see all the sons of Dhritarashtra, along with their allied kings, including Bhishma, Dronacharya, Karn, and also the generals from our side, rushing headlong into your fearsome mouths. I see some with their heads smashed between your terrible teeth. As many waves of the rivers flow rapidly into the ocean, so are all these great warriors entering into your blazing mouths. As moths rush with great speed into the fire to perish, so are all these armies entering with great speed into your mouths. O Vishnu, you are scorching the entire universe with the fierce, all-pervading rays of your effulgence.

Tell me, who are you in such a fierce form. O God of gods, I bow before you; please bestow your mercy on me. You, who existed before all creation, I wish to know who you are, for I do not comprehend your nature and your mission.

Lord reveals His Powers; verse 32 - 34

Hearing Arjun prayers, Lord Krishna said: I have come here to destroy all these warriors assembled for the war. Even without your participation in the war, all the warriors in the opposite army shall cease to exist. I have already destroyed all these; therefore, you get up and become merely the instrument and thus attain glory and enjoy a prosperous kingdom. Dronacharya, Bhishma, Jayadratha, Karn, and other brave warriors have already been killed by me. So kill all these great warriors without being disturbed. Do not fear. You will certainly conquer the enemies in the battle; therefore, fight!"

ARJUNA'S PRAYERS TO THE COSMIC FORM; verse 35 - 40

Hearing these words of Keshav, Sanjay tells Dhritrashtra (verse 35) that Arjun started trembling in fear. He prostrated with folded hands and spoke to Lord Krishna in faltering voice.

"O Master of the senses, it is but natural that the universe rejoices in giving you praise and is enamored by You. Demons flee fearfully from you in all directions and the saints bow to you. O great soul, you are the original creator of this world, you are even greater than Brahma, You are the Supreme Being. You are the ultimate resort of the entire universe; you are the knower, the object of knowledge, and the Supreme Abode who with infinite form pervade the entire universe."

"You are the fire god, the wind god, the water god and the moon god. You are the creator, as well as the father of the creator, and the controller of death. You are infinite might and valor, you pervade everything, and therefore you are everywhere and in everything. You are the father of this animate and inanimate world and the greatest guru to be worshipped. No one is even equal to you in the three worlds; how can there be one greater than you, who is of incomparable glory." Glorifying Lord Krishna in this way, Arjun bows down Him again and again.

Arjun asks for forgiveness; verse 41 - 46

Having seen the universal form of God, Arjun now felt regrets for the disrespect he thinks he may have shown toward Shri Krishna by audaciously looking upon Him as a mere friend. He is worried that due to his closeness with Him as a friend, and not knowing Him as God incarnation, he had addressed Him as "O Krishna," "O Yadav," "O my dear friend." So he implores forgiveness for whatever he may have done in forgetfulness of His divine personality.

Arjun again praises Shri Krishna in verse 43, "You are the father of the entire universe, of all moving and non-moving beings. You are the most deserving of worship and the supreme spiritual master. No one is even equal to you in all the three worlds, then who can possibly be superior to you, O possessor of incomparable power?"

Arjun then bows and prostrates in front of the Lord seeking His grace and asks Him to forgive him as a father tolerates his son. Arjun pleads and says, "Having seen your universal form that I had never seen before, I feel great joy. And yet, my mind trembles with fear. Please have mercy on me and again show me your pleasing form, O God of gods, O abode of the universe. O thousand-armed one, though you are the embodiment of all creation, I wish to see you in your four-armed form, carrying the mace and disc, and wearing the crown.

Lord Krishna resumes his human form (47- 51)

After seeing Arjun becoming fearful, Shri Krishna now pacifies him by explaining that there is no need to be scared. He had bestowed this divine vision of His universal form which no one else had seen it before, with the help of His Yogmaya. He declares that study of the Vedic texts, performance of ritualistic ceremonies, undertaking of severe austerities, abstinence from food, or generous acts of charity, all of these are not sufficient to bestow a vision of the cosmic form of God. This is only possible by his divine grace (Sanjay also received this vision by the grace of Ved Vyas, who is also considered to be an Avatar of God).

Sanjay tell Dhritrashtra that Lord Krishna thus pacifies Arjun and then appeared in front of him first in His four-armed form and then assumed His pleasant human form.

Seeing His gentle human form (two-armed), Arjun again bows to Lord Krishna and says that I have now regained my composure and my mind is restored to normal.

LORD CAN BE SEEN BY DEVOTIONAL LOVE (Verses 52 – 55)

Lord Krishna then said to Arjun, "this form of mine that you are seeing is exceedingly difficult to behold. Even the celestial gods are eager to see it. Neither by the study of the Vedas, nor by penance, charity, or fire sacrifices, can I be seen as you have seen me." However His two-armed form as he is standing before Arjun can only be realized through Bhakti. Devotion alone will unite us with God; devotion alone will help us see him; devotion alone will help us attain him; God is enslaved by true devotion, which is the best of all paths.

Shri Krishna concludes this chapter by highlighting five characteristics of those who are His true devotees and hence attain God.

- Those who perform all their duties for the sake of God alone
- Those who place their entire faith in His grace.
- Who behold Lord pervading all objects and personalities.
- Who are free of attachment
- Who are without malice toward all beings thinking that God resides in the heart of all beings and so they forgive even their wrongdoers.

- **HARI OM** –

Thus ends the Eleventh chapter entitled "VISHVRUP DARSHAN YOG"

CHAPTER 12 – THE YOGA OF DEVOTION

We have seen in the previous chapters that Arjun, though he had came prepared to the battle field to fight the war against Duryodhna and his sons, but just before the start of the war, he was overpowered by the thought that how can he kill his own people and great men like Bhishma and Dronacharya for whom he has great respect. He did not want to engage in such a battle where he will gain kingdom by killing his own family members. Instead, he thought of living a life of a saint and collect alms rather than gaining the kingdom and comforts.

Such a life style is possible for only two types of people – a Brahmchari or a Sanyasi. Arjun could not be a Brahmchari now, having married two times and having a grown up son. He could only become a Sanyasi and that is exactly what he thought also. He told Sri Krishna in so many words that he does not want kingdom after killing so many respected family members because it will not remove his sorrows. At the same time, he wanted the best for him and though he already had developed an inclination to follow the life of a Sanyasi, he requested Krishna to accept him as his disciple and teach him what is the best for him.

Lord Krishna first taught him the nature of Atma and then talked about Karm Yog saying that "you have choice only in doing action but not upon its results." Then Arjun wanted to know the characteristics of a wise person. Bhagvaan explained to him that the wise person is one who is happy within himself; nothing elates or depresses him like the water from all rivers entering the ocean which is already brimful, brings no change or disturbance in the ocean.

Arjun thus understood that Krishna wants him to gain knowledge because by knowledge alone he can be a wise man. He was wondering why Krishna is still asking him to fight this war. Due to this confusion, Arjun asked Shri Krishna in 3rd chapter that since you are praising knowledge to gain liberation, why you want me to engage in this dreadful action.

Lord Krishna does not give him a definite answer; he simply tells him what Karm Yog is and what Sanyas is. He says both are for gaining knowledge, difference is only in the life style - one is the life style of renunciation while the other is a life of activity with proper attitude which purifies the mind. Bhagvaan says, one cannot be a Sanyasi without being a Karm Yogi and therefore asks Arjun to be a Karm Yogi and explained in detail what Karm Yog is in the 3rd and 4th Chapters.

However, Arjun doubt still remained and that is why he again asked the same question in beginning of 5th Chapter. He asked "you praise both Karm Yog and Sanyas, please tell me definitely between the two which one is the best for me." In 3rd chapter, he had asked between Gyan and Karm Yog and later in 5th Chapter, he asks between Sanyas and Karm Yog, which is basically the same question but with different terminology.

Again Lord Krishna does not answer directly and simply says that what is achieved by the Sanyasi is also achieved by the Karm Yogi and both are same in true sense. A Karm Yogi does his duties towards family, society and his country with a mind of dedication to the Lord and meditates upon the human form of the Lord meaning Sagun Brahm. None of these duties exist for a Sanyasi, his life is one of dedicated pursuit for knowledge, nothing else and he meditates upon Nirgun Brahm, the Nirakar form, the Lord who is formless. A Sanyasi renounces all enjoined duties both what is to be done daily and what is to be done occasionally.

Having explained the distinction between the body and the soul and Karm Yog, Shri Krishna then describes the nature of Parmatma and the relationship between soul and God. One can attain liberation from the cycle of birth and death by God-Realization only. Then He explains that this divine knowledge and God Realization can be attained only through unflinching devotion to the supreme Lord. Finally Lord Krishna describes His glories in brief and then His cosmic Form.

Having seen the Cosmic Form of Bhagvaan in the 11th Chapter, Arjun asks the same question in 12th Chapter, in a slightly different way - which of the two groups of people is better? - Those who pursue Nirgun Brahm, God having no form or those who worship the Sagun Brahm, God in the various forms. Instead of asking the question in reference to their activity, Arjun framed the question in terms of worship, or meditation.

In 12th chapter, Lord Krishna emphasizes that the path of devotion is the highest among all types of spiritual practices. Practitioners of the spiritual path are also of two kinds—devotees of the formless Brahman, and devotees of Bhagvaan in His personal form. But the path of worshipping the formless is very difficult.

REASONS FOR WORSHIPPING A PERSONAL FORM OF GOD

Arjun asked Shri Krishna to tell him which of these two types has the best knowledge of yoga – those ever-steadfast devotees who worship you as in human form of Krishna, or those who worship the formless Absolute Supreme?

Devotees of Bhagvaan in human form are the best (verses 3- 7)

Lord Krishna said I consider the best yogis to be those who with steadfast devotion and faith and fixing their mind on me, worship the Supreme Lord having a human form.

Having said that worship of the personal form is the best, Shri Krishna clarifies that in no way does He reject the worship of the formless. Those who worship the formless aspect of Absolute Reality; the all-pervading, indefinable, imperishable, unmanifest, unthinkable, inconceivable, immovable and eternal Brahman, by restraining their senses and being even-minded everywhere, and engaged in the welfare of all beings, also attain God.

The path of Self-realization is more difficult for those who fix their mind on the invisible and formless Brahman because it is very difficult for human beings, having pride in the physical body, to comprehend someone who is invisible and formless or does not have a body.

(Why the worship of the formless Brahman is so difficult? The first and foremost reason for this is that we human beings possess a form ourselves and we have been habitual of interacting with others who have forms. Thus, we can easily focus our mind if we worship or meditate on someone whom we consider Bhagvaan. However, in the case of the formless, our intellect cannot conceive it, and the mind and senses have no tangible object to meditate upon.

The difference in paths can be understood through the logic of the baby monkey, and the logic of the baby kitten. The baby monkey clings onto her mother's stomach by itself unhelped by mother monkey. Baby monkey knows if it is unable to do so, it will fall down. In contrast, a kitten is helped by the mother cat by holding the kitten from behind the neck and lifting it up.

In this analogy, the devotees of the formless can be compared to the baby monkey and the devotees of the personal form can be compared to the baby kitten. Those who worship the formless Brahman have the onus of progressing on the path by themselves, because Brahman does not bestow grace upon them. Brahman is without attributes (nirviśheṣh), without qualities (nirguṇa), and without form (nirākār). Therefore, Brahman does not manifest the quality of grace. On the other hand, the personal form of God is an ocean of compassion and mercy. Hence, devotees of the personal form receive the help of divine support in their sādhanā.)

Therefore, the natural course for the ordinary seeker is to worship God having a form. The worship of God as a person in the form of one's personal favorite deity stimulates divine love that rouses Self-consciousness and experience of unity in due course of time.

Image worship is necessary in the beginning, but not afterwards, just as scaffolding is necessary during the construction of a building. A person must learn to fix thoughts and mind first on a personal God with a form and then, after succeeding therein, fix them upon the impersonal form. God quickly bestows His grace upon them and removes the obstacles on their path. For those who are in continuous communion with Him, He dispels their ignorance with the lamp of knowledge.

In this way, God Himself becomes the Savior of His devotees and liberates them from the cycle of life and death.

In fact, there is no real difference between the two paths — the path of devotion to a personal God and the path of Self-knowledge of the impersonal God in their higher reach. In the highest stage of realization they merge and become one.

Different ways of Bhakti - KARMA-YOGA is the best; Verses 8 - 12

In verse 8, Shri Krishna asks Arjun to fix the mind on God and also surrender the intellect to Him; only then you will always live in God. Why it is must to surrender the intellect to God while fixing the mind upon Him?

Lord is conveying here that mere physical devotion is not sufficient; we must absorb the mind in thinking of God; without the engagement of the mind, mere sensory activity is of no value. For example, we hear a sermon with our ears, but if the mind wanders off, the words will fall on the ears but they will not register in the mind and we will not remember what was said. The mind is such an instrument that in it, all the senses reside in the subtle form. Thus, even without the actual sensory activity, the mind experiences the perceptions of sight, smell, taste, touch, and sound. Therefore, while keeping count of our karmas, God keeps count of the mental thoughts also.

Even beyond the mind is the intellect. We can only fix the mind upon God when we surrender our intellect to Him. In material pursuits as well, when we face situations beyond the capability of our intellect, we take guidance from a person with superior intellect like we consult a doctor when we fall sick or engage a lawyer for a legal case etc. In the same way, at present our intellect is subject to many defects - we think of ourselves to be the perishable body; we think the material objects will always remain with us and hence we remain busy in accumulating them day and night. And though the pursuit of sensual pleasures only results in misery in the long run, we still chase them in the hope that we will find happiness.

If we run our lives in accordance with the directions of our intellect, we will definitely not make much progress on the divine path. Thus, if we wish to achieve spiritual success by attaching the mind to God, we must surrender our intellect to Him and follow His directions. Surrendering the intellect means to think in accordance with the knowledge received from God via the medium of the scriptures and the bonafide Guru.

Shri Krishna knew that it is not easy to fix the mind upon God. Therefore, He says in the **verse 9**, "keep practicing to remember Him with devotion. Each time the mind wanders toward other objects and ideas, strive to bring it back to God through remembrance of His Names, Forms, Virtues, abodes and so on." Practice makes the man perfect.

 Even the practice to remember God is also not easy. The mind is made from the material energy Maya and it naturally runs toward the material objects of the world.

When we get absorbed in our work, God slips out of the mind even if we had been trying to remember Him. So, Shri Krishna says in **verse 10**, "If you cannot practice remembering God with devotion, then just try to work for Him."

Whatever work one does, it should be done for the pleasure of the Lord as stated earlier also in verses 9.27 and 9.28. Living in this world, one should continue doing their duties towards the family, society and nation with attitude of surrendering all fruits of those actions to the Lord rather than doing it out of bodily attachment for them. In this way, by performing all actions for the exclusive satisfaction of Bhagvaan, our mind will become steady and we will soon be able to focus upon Him. Then, gradually love for God will manifest within the heart, and we will gain success in constantly thinking of Him.

If one is unable to even work for the pleasure of God in devotion, Shri Krishna gives them the fourth alternative in **verse 11**, and says to Arjun, "keep doing your works as before, but become detached from the fruits of your actions." Such detachment will purify our mind and intellect and then, the purified intellect will more easily be able to move ahead on the spiritual path.

Shri Krishna next says that the scriptural knowledge is better than mere ritualistic practice; meditation is better than scriptural knowledge; renunciation of selfish attachment to the fruits of work is better than meditation;

because mind gets purified immediately and strengthens the intellect to enable us to move on to the higher stage of Sadhna.

When one's knowledge of God increases, all Karmas are gradually eliminated because one who is situated in knowledge thinks he or she is not the doer but an instrument working at the pleasure of the creator. Such an action in dedication to God becomes devotion – free from any Karmic bondage. Thus, there is no sharp demarcation between the paths of selfless service, spiritual knowledge, and devotion.

Qualities of a Loving devotee (verses 13 – 19)

Krishna now describes in verses 13 to 19, the attributes of a devotee who is dear to Him. That devotee is most dear to God, who;

- Is free from malice towards all living beings even towards those who are inimical towards them.
- Is friendly and compassionate towards every one.
- Is free from attachment to possessions and egotism (pride).
- Has faith that only efforts are in his hands, while the results are in the hands of God. So whatever results come his way, he sees them as the will of God, and accepts them with equanimity.
- Is ever forgiving.
- Remains contented with whatever he gets.
- His mind is steadily united with God in devotion.

- Has mastery over his mind and senses and remains devoted to God with a firm resolve keeping mind and intellect always dwelling upon God.
- Is neither a source of annoyance to others nor gets agitated due to others wrong doing to him.
- Remains equal in pleasure and pain.
- is free from joy, envy, fear, and anxiety.
- Is indifferent to worldly gains.
- Remains pure internally as well as externally, skillful, remains untroubled whatever may be the outcome and rise above petty selfishness.
- Neither rejoices in mundane pleasures nor despair in worldly sorrows; neither hankers after pleasant worldly situations nor grieves in unpleasant ones.
- Renounces both good and evil actions. *(good actions here means ritualistic practices for material gains)*
- Is always full of devotion towards God.
- Remains the same towards friend or foe, in honour or disgrace, in heat or cold, in pleasure or pain.
- Avoids association with unfavorable people.
- Is indifferent to criticism or praise.
- Remains in silent contemplation of God.
- Remains content with whatever comes his ways.
- Is free from attachment to a place, a country, or a house;
- His intellect is firmly fixed on God with total devotion.

Shri Krishna then concludes this chapter telling Arjun, "those faithful devotees are exceedingly beloved to me who having complete faith in me set me as their ultimate goal and sincerely strive to develop the above mentioned nectar of moral values."

- **HARI OM** -

Thus ends the Twelfth chapter entitled "BHAKTI YOG"

CHAPTER 13 – CREATION AND CREATOR

The eighteen chapters of the Bhagavad Gita can be divided into three sections.

The first set of six chapters describe the Jeev, the soul, the Atma, situated in each body and the path of Karm Yog for God realization, knowing which one can be released from the cycle of birth and death.

The second set of six chapters from seven to twelve, describe the relationship between soul and supreme soul; Parmatma. The opulence and various glories of the God are also described and how one can attain His Grace by following the path of Bhakti or loving devotion of God.

The third set starting from chapter thirteen, expounds upon tattva gyāna or the oneness between Jeev and Parmatma.

In Chapter thirteen, Shri Krishna first starts with the theory of creation and the creator and what is real knowledge.

The human body or the creation is a replica of the universe. Whatever is here in the body is also there in the cosmos; in this chapter, Krishna tells Arjun that this body or whole creation is called the Kshetra, meaning field of activities, where you can reap the fruits of your actions depending upon the good or bad actions. And the person who knows this Kshetra is called Kshetragya –

the knower of all things or the creator. The human body is the medium by which the individual soul enjoys the material world, gets entangled, and in the end leaves that body to take birth in another form. The soul inside the body knows all the activities of its own body; it is, therefore, called the knower of the field of activities. The Lord knows all the bodies, whereas the individual soul knows only his own body. When one clearly understands the difference between the body, the individual soul inside the body, and the **Parmeshvar**, one is said to have real knowledge.

Parmeshvar is not just in one given body but in all the bodies, pervading the whole creation. When one Sun is reflected in many mirrors, though it looks like there are many Suns, but in reality there is only one Sun. Similarly, Parmeshvar is the only one creator who looks seemingly divided in various gods, humans, animals, microbes, trees, plants etc.

Chapter 13 begins with Arjun's question asking Lord Krishna to describe the three pairs of words - prakṛiti-puruṣh; kṣhetra-kṣhetragya and Gyan-Gyeya. Shri Krishna thus begins to explain the meaning of these three pairs of words; starting with kṣhetra-kṣhetragya first from second verse onwards.

Shri Krishna said; this body is called the **Kshetra** (the field of activities) and one who knows this body is called **Kshetragaya** (knower of the field). These two terms explain the distinction between the body and the soul.

The soul is distinct from the body-mind-intellect mechanism but due to ignorance of its divine nature, it identifies with these material entities. This body is the field of activities for the individual soul and because the soul is witness to all the activities of the body, it is called the Knower of the field.

The individual soul is the knower of the individual field of its own body; while God is the knower of the fields of all the souls in the entire world and therefore called the Supreme Soul or Parmatma; the knower of everything in the universe. Shri Krishna thus establishes the position of the three entities vis-à-vis each other - the material body, the soul, and the Supreme Soul. The entire world is the field of activities of Parmatma who is witness to all those activities of the world, while the individual body is the field of activities of the individual soul. **Therefore, the verse 3 of this chapter is called a Great Sentence, "In all the Kshetra, May you know me as Kshetragaya".** Understanding of the Self (Atma, soul), the Supreme Lord (the supreme soul, Parmatma) and the body, and the distinction amongst these, is true knowledge.

Shri Krishna further says; I will explain to you what that kshetra is and what its nature is. I will also explain how change takes place within it, from what it was created, who the knower of the field of activities is, and what his powers are. This knowledge has been sung by many saints and Rishis through different sentences in the Vedas which reveal the real nature of Parmeshvar in a very conclusive and convincing ways leaving no doubt at all.

Human body; the field of activities – verse 6 - 7

There are twenty-four elements that constitute the Human body or the field of activities. These are:

- Five gross elements (*paanch mahabhitah*) – earth, air, water, fire and sky.
- Five sense organs (nose, ears, tongue, eyes and skin)
- Five organs of actions (feet, hands, speech, anus and genitals)
- Five sense organs (smell, hear, see, speak and touch); also called *paanch tanmatras* produced by the *panchikaran kriya* of five gross elements.
- Mind (*mana*), Intellect (*Buddhi*) and Ego (*ahankara*) which together are called *antahkaran*.
- Unmanifest primordial matter (called *avyakt Prakriti* or fundamental quality)

Shri Krishna then elucidates the attributes of the kṣhetra (Body), and its modifications thereof:

i) The gross body in which the soul resides and which undergoes six transformations until death.

ii) Consciousness or the life force that exists in the soul, and which it also imparts to the body while it is present in it. This is just as fire has the ability to heat, and if we put an iron rod into it, the rod too becomes red hot with the heat it receives from the fire. Similarly, the soul makes the body seem lifelike by imparting the quality of consciousness in it.

iii) The Will or determination which is a quality of the intellect, and is energized by the soul.

iv) Desire (Ichha), which creates a longing for the acquisition of an object, a situation or a person, etc.

v) Aversion (Dvesh) which creates hatred for an object.

vi) Happiness that is experienced in the mind through fulfillment of desires.

vii) Sorrow or pain experienced in the mind when desires are not fulfilled.

In verse 8 - 12 Shri Krishna describe the **virtues, habits, behaviours, and attitudes** that purify the mind and illuminate it with the light of knowledge.

1 **Humbleness** (*amānitvam*), meaning refraining from self praise and not to demand respect from others for the knowledge he has. Though a person might be having many qualifications and may have achieved many awards for the good work done by him, but the problem comes when he starts demanding respect from others for his

accomplishments. A great scientist who is fretting and fuming because nobody recognized his work or accomplishments and he did not get a noble prize, is just a child since only children love to show off their accomplishments when others are watching. Maturity comes when you start respecting yourself in your own eyes and others respect you or not, is immaterial.

2 **Freedom from hypocrisy;** (adambhitvam) meaning that 'Not to declare one's own glories which one does not have and not to show pride for something which you do not possess or not to demand respect without having any qualification for it.' Do not show off your wealth, which does not belong to you but which you have borrowed from others or loaned from the bank.

3 **Non violence (***ahinsa***)** - Not hurting living beings including plants and trees. Do not deliberately, for your own sake, hurt another being. Ahinsa is an appreciation of pain of others and thus allows you to let other living beings live as they were meant to be. Ahinsa is a very dynamic word which has to be interpreted from time to time and situation to situation. There can be situations where you

have to destroy the evil like in case of a war as an example, Krishna himself asks Arjuna to rise and fight for Dharma and gain his kingdom.

4   Compassionate (kṣhānti) - Having composed mind that do not react orally or physically when he is harmed or abused in any way by someone. It also means having compassion and understanding towards others.

5   Simplicity (arjavam) - Straightforward person having alignment between thoughts, word and deeds. In other words, our actions must be consistent with our words and thoughts. If we say something but do something different or opposite, that is called crookedness. In simple words, speaking truth is a great quality of a wise person.

6   Having respect and love for the teacher or Guru and remaining connected with the Guru to have the knowledge with great devotion and faith in him.

7   Cleanliness or purity internally and externally (shaucham). External cleanliness begins with the

external environment, your dwelling place, physical body and cloths etc. Internal cleaning means purity of mind and thoughts so as not to have anger, greed, selfishness and hatred and so on. The internal cleaning can be achieved by prayers.

8   Steadfastness (sthairyam), remaining persistent in commitment to one's duties or path until the goal is reached.

9   Self control - restraining the mind and the senses from running after worldly pleasures that dirty the mind and intellect.

10   Dispassion towards sense pursuits and giving up longings. One may have desires but not the longing for fulfillment of the desires. It does not mean that one must have aversion to an object, but it simply means not to get attached to that object considering it as the only source of pleasure and happiness.

11   Absence of pride, absence of "I". "Me" and "mine" notions. One should not be arrogant for the virtues or wealth he has.

12   Remaining unaffected and unperturbed, not getting upset or unhappy in birth, death, old age, disease etc.

13   Absence of ownership, or not getting attached to his possessions. We must understand that everything has been given to us and because it has been given to us, it can be taken away any time. We can get rid of our attachment or sense of ownership by constantly looking at the fact that I only happen to possess few things, I am not the owner of anything. I am only a managing trustee of my body, mind and senses and few other things I am endowed with.

14   Absence of excessive affection towards son, wife, house etc. Love and care is fine but not more than that. When it becomes emotional dependence, it creates problems, sorrow and unpleasantness.

15. **Evenness of mind** in gain or loss of desirable and undesirables. Generally, if the situation is desirable, the mind is cheerful, and if not, it is sorrowful. The result of action is not in your hands and one should accept it as it comes whether it is according to your expectations or not. Accept it as Prasad of Ishvar.

16. Abiding and **unflinching devotion in God** and remain connected to the Lord, Ishvar, always.

17. Having inclination to live in a solitary and quiet place with natural environment like in mountains, large park or bank of a sacred river away from crowd of people.

18. Avoiding company of people engaged on worldly enjoyments who are a disturbance to your pursuits.

19. Consistency in dwelling upon the spiritual knowledge of Atma and Parmatma (Brahman)

20. Philosophical pursuit of the Absolute Truth - Only human beings are blessed with the faculty of knowledge. We should utilize this faculty to contemplate upon the questions: "Who am I? Why am I here? What is my goal in life? How was this world created? What is my connection with the Creator? How will I fulfill my purpose in life?" This contemplation will lead us to the divine knowledge or Atma gyan or God-Realization.

Summing up Bhagvaan says that all the above which have been told is knowledge because these are the means for gaining *gyan* and any thing opposite to this is ignorance (*agyan*).

Supreme Reality – verse 13 - 18

Shri Krishna then reveals to Arjun, 'what should be known (gyeyam) by knowing which, one attains immortality.' Shri Krishna then tells in a detail who is that to be known as Parmeshvar:

- It is the beginning less Brahman, who lies beyond existence and non-existence.
- The Brahman in Its formless and attribute less aspect, Bhagvaan in its human form and Paramātmā residing within the body, are three manifestations of the same Supreme Reality.
- He has hands and feet on all sides, eyes, head and face on all sides as well as ears on all sides because he is present in all the bodies in this world , he is all pervading, omnipresent and Witness of all that occurs in the three worlds. *(In other words, He accepts food offerings made to Him anywhere in the universe; He hears the prayers of His devotees, wherever they may be.)*
- He is the perceiver of all sense objects but does not have any physical sense organs. *(In other*

words, God does not possess material hands, feet, eyes, and ears. Yet He grasps, walks, sees, and hears)*
- He is the sustainer of creation, and yet detached from it. *(In His form as Lord Vishnu, God maintains the entire creation. He sits in the hearts of all living beings, notes their karmas, and gives the results. Under Lord Vishnu's dominion, Brahma manipulates the laws of material science to ensure that the universe functions stably. Also, under Lord Vishnu's dominion, the celestial gods arrange to provide the air, earth, water, rain, etc. that are necessary for our survival. Hence, God is the Sustainer of all. Yet, He is complete in Himself and is, thus, detached from everyone. The Vedas mention Him as ātmārām, meaning "one who rejoices in the self and has no need of anything external.)*
- He is devoid of the three gunas, and yet the enjoyer of the three Gunas by becoming the living entity.
- He is inside as well as outside of all living beings, those that are moving or not moving. He is present in all living beings as well as in the entire universe. (He is all pervading)
- He is most subtle that cannot be seen by any one just as one cannot see the water present in the

Sun rays. *(God is not knowable by the senses, mind, and intellect.)*
- He is very near because He resides in one's inner self as well as far away in the Supreme Abode because no one can reach there.
- He is undivided, yet appears to exist as if divided in all living beings. For example one planet earth appears divided into so many countries; one country appears divided into several states; one state appears divided into districts, and so on, similarly, one Reality appears divided in numerous infinite forms. The reflection of the Sun in puddles of water appears divided, and yet the Sun remains indivisible. These are apparent divisions because they have the same order of reality.
- God is Creator, the Maintainer, and the Destroyer of everything. Just as the ocean throws up waves and then absorbs them back into itself, similarly God creates the world, maintains it, and then absorbs it back into Himself.
- God makes all things luminous; it is by His luminosity that all luminous objects give light. *By His radiance, the sun and moon become luminous. In other words, the luminosity of the Sun and the moon is borrowed from God.*
- He is said to be beyond darkness of ignorance. He is true knowledge (gyana), the object of knowledge

(gyeya), and the goal of knowledge (gyana-gamya).
- He dwells within the hearts of all living beings.

Shri Krishna says that thus, I have briefly described creation, as well as knowledge and the object of knowledge. Understanding this, my devotee attains My Supreme Abode.

Prakriti and Purush and their interaction; verse 20- 24

In next few verses, Lord Krishna explains the relation between *Prakriti and Purush*.

Prakriti is material Nature of God consisting of three Gunas and also called Maya while *Purush* is individual soul or Jeevatma and while God Himself is called *Param Puruśh* (the Supreme Living Entity). *Prakriti* has potential to create everything, not alone but with the *Purush (the supreme soul)* which provides the very existence of creation. Therefore, *Prakriti* also is beginning less since being energy of God; it has existed ever since God existed.

Together as *Ishvar*, these two are the causes. Though both have the status of being the cause, *Purusha* is the basis of *Prakriti* which is also called God's Maya.

Various changes in the body from birth till death are brought about by Prakriti which also creates the three modes of nature - sattva, rajas, and Tamas and their countless varieties of combinations. The Material Energy or Prakriti is thus responsible for all the cause and effect in the world. *The Vedas state that there are 8.4 million species of life in the material world.*

The individual soul (Jeev) gets a bodily form according to its past karmas, and it identifies itself with the body, mind, and intellect. Thus, it seeks the pleasure of the bodily senses. Since the body is made of Maya, it seeks to enjoy the material world having three guṇas - mode of goodness, mode of passion, and mode of ignorance.

The senses, mind, and intellect are energized by the soul and they work under its dominion and thus perform all the activities. Due to the ego, the soul identifies itself as the doer and the enjoyer of the body. Just as if a bus meets with an accident, the wheels and the steering are not blamed for it but the driver is held accountable. Similarly, the individual soul accumulates all the karmas performed by the body-mind-intellect complex. This stockpile of karmas, accumulated from innumerable past lives, is the cause of birth of the human being in good and evil wombs.

Shri Krishna has thus explained the status of the jīvātmā (individual soul) within the body. In verse 23, He explains the position of the Paramātmā (Supreme Soul), who also resides within the human body. The individual soul remains unaffected by the Prakriti as the sun's reflection in water is unaffected by the properties of water. However the individual soul, forgetting its real nature, associates with the six sensory faculties and ego of the body and becomes attached, performs good and evil deeds, loses independence and transmigrates as a living entity as individual soul.

In earlier verse of this chapter, we have also learnt that individual soul is the knower of the individual body while the Supreme Soul is the knower of all the infinite bodies.

In this verse 23, Shri Krishna says, "The Supreme Soul also resides in the hearts of all living beings as the Paramātmā. Seated within, He notes their actions, keeps an account of their karmas, and bestows the results at the proper time, keeping it in the cycle of birth and death." The Parmatma always watches the jīvātmā (individual soul) to whatever body it receives in each lifetime.

(In the Muṇḍakopaniṣhad, this is beautifully explained by giving an example of two birds seated in the nest (heart) of a tree (the body). The two birds represent the jīvātmā (individual soul) and Paramātmā (Supreme Soul). The jīvātmā has its back toward the Paramātmā, and is busy enjoying the fruits of the tree (the results of the karmas it receives while residing in the body). When a sweet fruit comes, it becomes happy; when a bitter fruit comes, it becomes sad. The Paramātmā is a friend of the jīvātmā, but He does not interfere; He simply sits and watches. If the jīvātmā can only turn around to the Paramātmā, all its miseries will come to an end." The jīvātmā has been bestowed with free will i.e. the freedom to turn away or toward God. By the improper use of that free will the jīvātmā is in bondage, and by learning its proper usage, it

can attain the eternal service of God and experience infinite bliss.)

Those who understand the truth about these three entities in creation - the ever changing material nature, the individual souls, and the master of both (the Supreme soul- Parmatma) along with its three modes of nature will not take birth here again. They will be liberated regardless of their present condition.

In verses 25 & 26, Shri Krishna then describes some of the **spiritual practices** followed by human beings in their pursuit for Self Realization.

- Some aspirants are attracted to meditating upon God seated within their hearts. They relish the spiritual bliss that they experience when their mind comes to rest upon the Lord within them.
- Some try to go through the cultivation of knowledge about the three entities - soul, Parmatma, and Maya through the processes of hearing (śhravaṇa), contemplating (manan), and Deep Meditation (nididhyāsan) with firm faith.
- Yet some others follow the path of action with the attitude of Karm Yog with full faith and devotion in the service of God.
- There are still others who are unaware of these spiritual paths, but somehow, they hear the knowledge through saints and sages, and then get drawn to the spiritual path and begin worshipping the Supreme Lord. By such devotion to hearing

from saints, they too can gradually cross over the ocean of birth and death.

Shri Krishna tells Arjun in verse 27 that all living things whatsoever existing, mobile or immobile, are born because of the union of **Kshetra (field of activities)** and **Kshetragya (knower of the field)** or Anatma and Atma. In other words, all life forms are the combination of the eternal soul, which is the source of consciousness, and the body, which is made of the insentient material energy.

Shri Krishna tells in verse 28 that those who perceive the Paramātmā (Supreme Soul) also seated within all the human bodies along with the Individual Soul (Jeevatma), as well as clearly understand that the Atma and Parmatma are imperishable and the Supreme Soul accompanies the individual soul as it travels from body to body in the cycle of life and death, only they clearly see and are true *Gyani*. Although the living beings perish but the Atma and Parmatma remain same and do not perish. The body dies, the mind dies as the thoughts keep dying one after the other, the whole time bound existent world dies, but the Atma and the Parmatma remain always existent.

When one beholds the same Supreme soul existing equally everywhere and in all living beings, he will not hate or harm anybody because he considers every being as one's own self. Seeing everyone as a part of God, they maintain a healthy attitude of respect and service toward others. He naturally refrains from mistreating, cheating, or insulting others, when he perceives in them the presence of God. Thus, he elevates his mind by seeing God in all living beings, and finally attains the Supreme Abode.

He truly sees and understands that all actions are being performed by **Prakriti** alone in all ways while the Atma sitting inside actually does nothing, and therefore does not consider himself as the doer.

There are numerous forms of life in existence, from the tiniest amoeba to the most powerful celestial gods. All of them are rooted in the same reality - the soul, which is a part of God, seated in the body, which is made from the material energy. The moment we see the diverse variety of beings all rooted in one Parmatma only and coming out from that alone, then it will immediately lead us to the Brahman realization.

The God situated within the heart of all living beings as supreme soul, never identifies with the body, neither does anything nor gets affected by results of its actions. He has no beginning and is without any attributes.

Just as space holds everything within it, but being subtle, does not get contaminated by what it holds. Similarly, the soul retains its divinity even while it pervades the body as consciousness and thus the soul is not affected by the attributes of the body.

Just as one Sun, situated at one place illumines the entire solar system, so does the individual Atma seated in the heart spreads its consciousness throughout the field of the body. Similarly, the one Supreme Soul, the Parmatma, energizes all the living beings in the entire universe

In last verse 35, Shri Krishna winds up the topic of the field and the knower of the field by summing up all that He has said. True knowledge is to know the distinction between the Body (the field of activity- Kshetra) and the knower of the field of activity (Kshetragya). Those who know this distinction through the eyes of wisdom and also know their true nature as soul; sat chit Anand and as tiny parts of God, they seek the path of spiritual elevation and release from the trap of divine illusory Maya. Thus treading on the path of spiritual enlightenment, such persons of wisdom attain their ultimate goal of God-Realization.

- **HARI OM -**

Thus ends the "Thirteenth chapter entitled KSHETR KSHETRAGY VIBHAG YOG"

CHAPTER 14 – DIVISION OF THREE GUNAS

In the thirteenth chapter, Shri Krishna explained the difference between the material body, the soul and the Supreme soul in detail. In this chapter, He explains the nature of His material energy, which is the source of the body and its elements. The material nature constitutes of three gunas - sattva (goodness), rajas (passion), and Tamas (ignorance). Since the body, mind, and intellect are material in nature, they too possess these three modes, and a combination of these gunas forms the basis of one's character.

Guna in Sanskrit means rope and rope is used to tie up things, therefore, these three gunas are the cause of our bondage with the body and the world in general.

Peacefulness, morality, well-being, serenity, etc. are the virtues of those in the mode of goodness. Those driven by passion have endless desires and ambitions; they strive to satiate them and work towards worldly enhancement. However, those in the mode of ignorance; are gripped by laziness, excessive sleep, delusion, intoxication, and other vices. A spiritual seeker needs to deal with all these three immensely powerful forces of material nature. Once the soul is able to transcend above these three modes, it attains illumination. To break free from the clutches of these gunas, Shri Krishna reveals a simple solution to Arjun, which is to attach his mind to God.

Shri Krishna begins this chapter by telling Arjun in verses 1 & 2, "I shall once again explain to you the supreme wisdom, the best of all knowledge; by knowing which, all the great saints have attained the highest perfection. Those who take refuge in this wisdom will be united with me. They will not be reborn at the time of creation nor destroyed at the time of dissolution."

'United with God' means that once this true knowledge is realized the wise Gyani will acquire "a similar divine nature" as God himself.

When the soul is released from the bondage of the material energy, it comes under the dominion of God's divine Yogmaya energy. The divine energy equips it with God's divine knowledge, love, and bliss. As a result, the soul becomes of the 'nature of God' - it acquires 'divine godlike qualities'.

The cause of the entire world – verse 3 & 4

We all know that for a child to be born, a mother and father is required, similarly in the cause of the world, there is an intelligent cause and a material cause (known as Prakriti).

As the child is born to the mother, similarly Prakriti is the material cause out of which this creation is born. But the mother cannot produce a child without a father and so too, Prakriti requires an efficient cause. As for a child, for this entire creation too, two causes are required.

We now know one cause of this creation that is the material cause known as Prakriti or Maya from which all forms including even gods, manes, human beings, domestic animals and wild animals etc. are born. Then what is the intelligent cause of this universe?

Lord Krishna says in 4th verse that "I am the father of all these creatures who gives the seed in various wombs in which these forms are born". In Śhrīmad Bhāgavatam also, it is said, "In the womb of the material energy the Supreme Lord impregnates the souls. Then, inspired by the karmas of the individual souls, the material nature gets to work to create suitable life forms for them."

Prakriti itself has no real existence without God who lends existence and consciousness to it. This combination of Parmatma, Atma and Prakriti has omniscience and omnipotence and is the cause of the whole creation.

The three Gunas of Human beings (Verse 5 – 13)

Shri Krishna now explains in the next nine verses how Prakriti binds the individual soul.

The material energy (Prakriti) consists of three guṇas - sattva (goodness), rajas (passion), and Tamas (ignorance). Hence the body, mind, and intellect that are made from *Prakriti* also possess these three gunas. These gunas bind the eternal individual souls to the respective perishable body.

These three Gunas are not attributes of a person but these are very nature of Prakriti which explain certain conditions we experience in our daily life. Each of these Gunas is different from each other, as each type of gem. Every gem is a precious stone, but there is a difference between each gem - a Sapphire is different than an Emerald.

All the three guṇas are present in our mind as well. They can be compared to three wrestlers competing with each other. Each keeps throwing the others down, and so, sometimes the first is on top, sometimes the second, and sometimes the third. In the same manner, the three guṇas keep gaining dominance over the individual's temperament, which oscillates amongst the three modes. Depending upon the external environment, the internal contemplation, and the sanskārs (tendencies) of past lives, one or the other guṇa begins to dominate. There is no rule for how long it stays - one guṇa may dominate the mind and intellect for as short as a moment or for as long as an hour.

No one is endowed with only one guna as we see that even the Tamsic person has knowledge and therefore enjoys predominance of Satvic, though occasionally.

When you are cheerful, happy, and content and inclined towards spirituality, *sattva guṇa* is more predominant. When *rajo guṇa* becomes predominant, we become passionate, agitated, ambitious, envious of others success, and develop a gusto for sense pleasures.

When *tamo guna* becomes prominent, we become dull, lethargic, and inactive and come under the influence of anger, resentment and violence.

As said before, all these three *gunas* are present in all human beings. However at any time, one of these Gunas is predominant overwhelming the other two:

- *Sattva guna* is predominant while suppressing *rajo guna* and *tamo guna*.
- *Rajo guna* is predominant suppressing *sattva guna* and *tamo guna* and.
- *Tamo guna* becomes predominant suppressing *sattva guna* and *rajo guna*.

When sattva guna manifests in your body and sense organs, there is light of awareness in the whole body and mind giving a feeling of happiness all around. Action born out of sattva guna will be in accordance with Dharma and thus, will bear good results devoid of distress, earning Puny. As a result of these good actions, we will enjoy life free from pain in this life and next life as well.

When *rajo guna* is predominant, it gives rise to greed and desire. Once greed develops our thinking changes to justify it. Another manifestation of *rajo guna* is meaningless activity like moving restlessly, making knots and nail biting and so on. The desire puts you into action to earn more money, gain power and accumulate all wealth at any cost. The absence of tranquility i.e. mental restlessness is another manifestation of *rajo guna*. It can even be a creative restlessness. The result of actions born out of *rajo guṇa* pravriti is pain. A person who is impelled by *rajo guṇa*, is under great pressure and because of that he cannot always follow the right means, and thus some wrong action will be unavoidable due to which he will have lot of discomforts in life.

When tamo guna becomes predominant, there is absence of alertness and discrimination and total indifference towards performing any activity. Also delusion develops, either the mind is not capable of thinking or if it is, it draws erroneous conclusions.

We get what we deserve is God's law, the law of karma; verse 14 - 15

Shri Krishna explains that the destiny awaiting each Jeevatma is based upon the guṇas of their personalities.

Those who had predominance of sattva are born in families of pious people, scholars or higher celestial abodes.

Those who die with prevalence of greed and worldly ambitions are born among people driven by intense material activity like business class families.

While those who were inclined to intoxication, violence, laziness, and dereliction of duty, take birth in the families of illiterate people or they may descend down the evolutionary ladder by being born into the animal species.

The actions performed by persons under the influence of sattva guna are good and virtuous actions and therefore the fruits of their actions are uplifting and satisfying. The actions of those influenced by rajas guna are done with the intention of sense-gratification for themselves and their dependents. Therefore, these actions lead them to pain and sorrow. While those who are predominated by Tamas guna commit sinful deeds to relish perverse pleasures, which result in further delusion and ignorance for them.

Having mentioned the variation in the results that accrue from the three gunas, Shri Krishna gives the reason for this in verse 17. Sattva guna gives rise to wisdom, which confers the ability to discriminate between right and wrong. It also pacifies the desires of the senses for gratification, and creates a concurrent feeling of happiness and contentment. People influenced by it are inclined toward intellectual pursuits and virtuous ideas. Thus, the satva guna promotes wise actions. Rajo guna inflames the senses, and puts the mind out of control, sending it into a spin of greed. Tamo guna covers the person with inertia and senselessness and thus performs wicked and impious deeds.

Those who are in sattva guna reach the higher celestial abodes; those who are in rajo guna return to the earth planet; and those who are in tamo guna go to the lower worlds.

All the living beings are under the grip of these three guṇas, and hence all the works done by human beings in this world are due to these guṇas.

Shri Krishna tells in verse 19 & 20, the simple way for coming out of the bondage from the gunas of Prakriti or material nature.

All the living entities in the world are under the grip of the three guṇas, and hence the guṇas are the active agents in all the works being done in the world. But the Supreme Lord is beyond them. Therefore, those who know God to be beyond the three gunas, they attain the divine nature of God. Shri Krishna further explains that when one transcends the three modes of material nature associated with the body, then Maya no longer binds the living being and one becomes free from birth, old age, disease and death and attains immortality.

Arjun's question – verse 21

Hearing this, Arjun asked the characteristics of those who have transcended the three guṇas. In what manner do they conduct themselves and how one can get rid of these three gunas of Prakriti knowing that these gunas exist in Prakriti, the cause of this creation that manifest in our body-mind-sense complex.

First let us understand the meaning of transcending the three gunas; known as *'gunateet'*. Assume that you are sitting on the roof of your house and there is an open van full of flowers or full of garbage passing by on the road below. You don't get affected by any of these since these are happening far away from your house and thus do not affect you at all. Similarly, if we realize that my real nature is not the body, but I am Atman, then you will find that whatever is happening belongs to my body only and does not affect my inner self, in any way. Once you realize this, you will remain unperturbed under spell of gain or loss, pain or happiness, summer or winter, or when you are overactive or lazy. This state of realization means that you have risen above all the gunas. Whatever is happening is the role of Prakriti through your gross body. A wise person, who has risen above all the three Gunas, is called a Gunateet.

But to reach this stage is not so simple. We know that earth attracts all objects towards it due to earth gravity, as long as we are within earth atmosphere. When we rise above earth atmosphere, we come out of earth gravity region, but may come under the gravity of moon or other planets. Similarly, as long as we are under the influence of Prakriti or Maya, we get attracted towards the three gunas of Prakriti.

Tamoguna has highest attractive power, followed by rajoguna and lowest attraction power in satvguna. Then how we can come out of the attractive power of the Prakriti or Maya and rise above the gunas.

Shri Krishna answers the three questions of Arjuna: verses 22 - 25

First in verses 22 & 23, Shri Krishna describes the characteristics of a gunateet.

Shri Krishna explains that a person, who has risen above the three modes of Prakriti, is neither miserable nor jubilant when the modes of nature perform their natural functions in the world. When he experiences pleasure and happiness, he knows Satv is responsible for it. He is neither repulsed nor attracted by these experiences because of very clear understanding that they are all products of the gunas.

When he finds restlessness and an inclination to pursue activity, he knows that this is only effect of Rajas. And when he experiences confusion or dullness, he knows that Tamas has become predominant and makes no conclusion about him.

He is not anxious about any particular state of mind. He knows that he is SAT CHIT ANAND. He remains neutral to what all is happening around him. He is merely a witness. Take an example - when two people are arguing, a third person who is just watching without joining either side, he is simply a witness, indifferent to both views without any opinion to offer.

Shri Krishna then explains in verses 24 & 25, how a gunateet conducts in various situations. He says, "A wise person is unaffected and remains same when there is pain or happiness, by pleasant or unpleasant incident, or with reference to a clod of earth, a stone or gold. He is not affected also with reference to praise or insult, friend or enemy. All his actions and pursuits are not for personal glory but for benefit of others."

In the last two verses of this chapter, Bhagvaan reveals the one and only method of transcending these modes of material nature. Shri Krishna says that only those who serve me with love and unwavering devotion rise above these three gunas and reach the abode of God. The all-powerful God has both aspects to his personality- the formless and the personal form. God in His personal form as Krishna is the basis of formless, immortal and imperishable Brahman, everlasting Dharma and absolute divine bliss (Param Anand). Shri Krishna thus unequivocally confirms that the only way to rise above the three gunas is to engage in unwavering devotion to the personal form of the Supreme Lord.

- **HARI OM** -

Thus ends the "Fourteenth chapter entitled GUNTRAY VIBHAG YOG"

Nothing exists permanently

- Every one has to leave this world, even though he wishes not to. No magic can actually help a person to stay forever
- Everyone has their set life periods. One who is born, will die one day and will be born again according to his Karmas.

God is the cause of this creation

- Krishna is the incarnation of God, Parmatma or Ishvar by whatever name we call Him.
- God alone is the original cause of all causes.
- He starts everything and ends everything too.
- He is there everywhere. He is omnipresent and omnipotent
- We are just puppets whom he controls.

CHAPTER 15 - PURUSHOTAM YOGA

Shri Krishna had enlightened Arjun in the previous chapter that by transcending the effects of the three gunas, one can achieve the divine goal. And unflinching devotion to God is the best means of transcending beyond these gunas. Such devotion is practiced by detaching the mind from the world and attaching it to God alone.

The fifteenth chapter of the Bhagavad Gita is unique in several respects. It is the shortest, with only twenty verses. On the other hand, it summarizes the entire essence of not just the Gita but also all the Vedas in those twenty shlokas. Specifically, it covers four topics - the world, the individual soul (described as jeev or Jeevatma in Vedas), its root causes the God, and the relationship between Jeev, the world and God.

Thus the whole knowledge to be known by Vedas has been presented briefly and completely in Chapter 15. After explaining the nature of God in previous chapters 7 - 12, Shri Krishna now describes God as the source of everything in the world and present everywhere in His creation. Atma is everything, and beyond that Atma within every human being, there is Supreme Lord who sustains this whole world, who is the brilliance in the Sun, Moon and Fire, who blesses all plants with nutrients, and essence of food, who knows everything and He is one who is non-perishable as well as changeless. The Supreme Divine Personality, who is the eternal source, sustainer, and regulator of the entire world, is called Purushottam or God.

All the souls (Jeevatma) in this world are His eternal fragments, and hence they too are divine. However, they come under the influence of material nature and engage into all sorts of activities through their six senses, including the mind. The individual soul, ignorant of its divine nature, savors the material objects of the senses and at the time of death, it carries with it the mind and senses; from the present and previous lives. The ignorant person identifies himself with the body-mind-intellect and can neither perceive the presence of the soul in the body when alive nor its departure upon death. This is how the Jeevatma keep growing its bondage in the material world.

Lord Krishna reveals that, by recognizing the glories of God that shine forth all around in this world, the Yogis see this process clearly with the eyes of knowledge and purity of their minds.

Shri Krishna compares this Human body and the world with an upside down Ashwatth tree (verse 1 & 2)

In the first shloka, the vision of the human body and the universe is presented through imagination of an upside down peepal tree. Lord Krishna said: The universe (or human body) may be compared to an eternal Aśhvatth tree which is an upside-down peepal (sacred fig) tree that has its origin (or root) in the Supreme Lord, nourished and supported by Him. *(Aśhvatth also means; which will not remain the same even on the next day or something which is constantly changing.)* The trunk and branches which are extending downwards encompass all the life-forms existing on the earth. The Vedic hymns (rituals) are the leaves of this tree which protects this tree and helping it to grow.

One who truly understands this tree, its origin, its nature and working is a knower of the Vedas in a true sense.

Lord Krishna then explains how the human form is similar to the aśhvatth tree. The branches of this eternal tree extend both upwards and downwards and thus are spread all over the cosmos in the form of various gods, human beings, animals, birds and insects etc. The three modes of material nature or the three gunas irrigate this eternal tree of material existence. The sense pleasures generated by these gunas are like buds on the tree, which sprout into aerial roots as they evoke desires of bodily pleasures in a person. To satiate these desires, the human being performs Karm. But these desires are unending and keep increasing similar to the aerial roots, causing Karmic bondage, which keep the human beings bound with this cosmic tree due to which they have to take birth again and again.

Only the human being has the right to do new actions while all other species have to experience the results of their past karmas.

The beginning, the end, or the real form of this tree is not directly visible for the human beings on the earth. We can see the tree standing, but cannot see its roots because of which the tree exists. We recognize the existence of roots because of the existence of tree; similarly, the root of the world is beyond our comprehension. We do not see it but we infer its existence because of observation of the world. In other words, we see only the effect, but not the cause and infer the existence of cause from the presence of the effect. We can't see the cause since it is within ourselves beyond time and space. As a tree has roots which we cannot see, so is the world whose roots are hidden in the seer.

Remedy for endless sufferings of human beings; (verses 3 – 5)

The only way to rid ourselves of these endless sufferings is 'asaṅg' which means detachment. The axe of detachment can cut the roots of desires which are nourished by the three modes of material nature. With detachment, one can stop further growth of the tree roots, and due to lack of nourishment, the tree starts to wither.

The Lord further explains that this axe of detachment can only be developed with the knowledge of the Self. One has to realize that, "I am not this material body, but an eternal spiritual being. The everlasting happiness that I pursue cannot be achieved with material things. My endeavors towards gratification of the material desires of this material body have no satiation; they are only getting me further trapped in the sansaar or the web of life and death."

The next step to cultivate dispassion is to go straight to the source of this upside-down tree, which in real terms is on the top and much higher than everything else. It is here that the Supreme Lord of all creation resides. Having cut the firm roots of the desires of this tree, one should seek the Supreme Lord. To find the ultimate source, we must totally surrender to God and take refuge in Him. By doing this, we will not return to this material world and after death will go to His divine Abode.

Shri Krishna further says that only the liberated personalities reach that eternal abode who are free from pride and delusion, who have conquered the evil of attachment, who constantly dwell in the Supreme Being with all lust completely stilled, and who are free from dualities of pleasure and pain.

The nature of eternal abode; verse 6

Shri Krishna says that my Supreme Abode is self luminous and cannot be illumined by any other source like the Sun or the moon, or the fire. Having reached there, people attain permanent liberation (Mukti) and do not come back to this temporal world. The eternal Abode exists even after everything gets dissolved into unmanifest Nature during complete dissolution.

The Individual soul is part of Supreme Soul; part of Parmatma; (verse 7 – 9)

Shri Krishna then addresses the state of the jeev, the individual soul. From an absolute standpoint, there is only one eternal essence, one consciousness, and one supreme Soul, one Parmatma. But just as space seems like it is divided into many through walls, this eternal essence is as though divided into multiple souls through different bodies. The individual soul (Jeevatma) in the body of living beings associates with the six sensory faculties of perception including the mind and activates them. Just as the air takes aroma away from the flower, similarly the individual soul takes the six sensory faculties of perception, intellect, ego and five vital forces from one physical body to the new physical body it acquires after death.

The wind is neither affected nor unaffected by association with dust or aroma; similarly the individual soul called the subtle body is neither affected nor unaffected by association with the physical body. The subtle body carries the individual's good and bad Karmas of this life and past lives, to the next life till all Karmas are exhausted. But the human being in the new body picks up new desires and takes up yet another human body once the old one ceases to function.

In Verse 10 & 11, Shri Krishna says that the ignorant person do not perceive the soul residing in the body and presume physical body to be the self. Only those individuals who have the eye of wisdom, who have assimilated the teaching of the scriptures after purifying themselves with Karm Yog and Bhakti Yog, recognize the non-divided nature of the Self. Without the soul, the body is lifeless. When the soul departs, consciousness ends.

Paramatma is the essence of everything; (Verses 12 – 15)

The third topic, the nature of God or Ishvar, is taken up next. We learn that Ishvar is not some remote figure, but pervades every aspect of the universe. Ishvar provides awareness or the faculty to know.

In verse 12, Lord Krishna explains that the entire creation is the manifestation of God's energy. The Sun gets its brilliance from Him. (According to scientific theories, the energy emitted by the sun every second is equivalent to millions of nuclear power plants put together. This has been an uninterrupted process for billions of years, yet it has not reduced in any way. The glory and brilliance of the sun is a part of God's wonderful creation.) Similarly, the radiance of the moon and the energy of fire are from Him only.

Shri Krishna next says, "Permeating the earth, I support and nourish all living beings with My energy. This energy is circulated throughout the universe in the form of nectar, providing nourishment to all the plants with the juice of life." It is His energy which has brought about the appropriate physical conditions for life to exist on planet earth. Like all other celestial bodies, the earth is also a big mass of matter. But God has made it habitable, so that, it can sustain life. (Ever wondered, why ocean water is so salty? God could have made the oceans full of fresh water, but it would have become a breeding ground for diseases. Due to the high salt content of the ocean water, many disease-causing microorganisms cannot survive in it, thereby protecting life.)

God exists inside all living beings as vaiśhvānara, meaning "fire of digestion," which is ignited by the power of God and uniting with vital breaths, digests all the four types of food." In Bṛihadāraṇyak Upaniṣhad also it is stated; "God is the fire inside the stomach that enables living beings to digest food." Shri Krishna has mentioned about four types of food in verse 14; Bhojya - Foods that are chewed, such as bread, chapatti, etc.; Peya - These are mostly liquid or semi-solid foods which we have to swallow or drink, such as milk, juice, etc.; Kośhya - Foods that are sucked, such as sugarcane and Lehya - This includes foods that are licked, such as honey, etc.

Lord Krishna further says; that seated in the hearts of all living beings (in the Intellect), God has bestowed upon human beings the amazing ability of memory, knowledge, as well as forgetfulness of the past. All the Vedas give knowledge about the God only; He alone is the author of the Vedānt, and the knower of the meaning of the Vedas. (The Kaṭhopaniṣhad states: All the Vedic mantras are actually pointing towards God.)

Relationship between Soul and Parmatma (verse 16 – 19)

The fourth topic deals with relationship between the individual, the world, and God.

Shri Krishna says that there are two entities in the cosmos: The changeable and perishable creation including all living and nonliving beings, fourteen planetary spheres down to a blade of grass. And there are unchangeable; imperishable individual souls called in Vedanta as Jeevatma. All created beings are subject to change, but the soul does not change.

Besides these is the Supreme Divine Personality, called the Paramatma, which means the Supreme Soul. While the individual soul is very tiny and confined to the material body it resides in; the Supreme Soul is present inside every living entity. He enters the three worlds as the unchanging controller and supports all living beings. He is the constant companion of the individual soul in every life, immaterial of what species the soul gets born into. He sits in their hearts quietly taking a note; keeping an account of their karmas, and gives appropriate results. The Supreme Soul also exists in a personal form as the four-armed commonly known as "Bhagvaan Vishnu" who has taken avatar as Krishna.

Shri Krishna says in verse 18, "I am also called Puruṣhottam, the Divine Supreme Person who transcends over the material world, which includes both the perishable physical bodies (kṣhar) and the imperishable divine souls (akṣhar)." The Vedas and the Smritis have described Him similarly. (*Lord Vishnu, Lord Shiva, and all the other Gods and Goddesses are different manifestations of the same Bhagvaan, the Supreme Divine Personality.*)

The wise person knows that there is only one Supreme Entity that manifests in three ways in the world - Brahman, Paramātmā, and Bhagvaan. God is one, and these forms are only His manifestations. As water exists in nature as ice, water, and steam that have different physical properties; but are forms of the same substance; likewise, God exists in these three forms. As Brahman, the infinite energies of God are all latent. He merely displays eternal knowledge and bliss. As Paramātmā, the Supreme Soul, he resides in the hearts of all living creatures. And as Bhagvaan, He manifests all His energies and sustains the entire universe. Those who seek God as Bhagvaan, the Supreme Divine Personality can truly acquire complete knowledge of Him.

If we trace the energy source of a tiny mango sapling, and of a 100 megawatt solar power plant, we reach the same source – the sun. Similarly, if we mentally remove the apparent limitations, the titles, the names and forms behind the individual and the world, we find the same pure unadulterated eternal essence. It is beyond the perishable visible world and the imperishable seed of the visible world. In other words, we learn that the Atma in us is the Atma in everyone, the Self of all.

Shri Krishna concludes this chapter by telling Arjun that I have thus given you the gist of all the hidden knowledge of the Vedic Scriptures. Having understood this, one becomes enlightened, one's all duties are accomplished, and the goal of human life is achieved.

- HARI OM -

Thus ends the Fifteenth chapter entitled "PURUSHOTAM YOG"

Nothing exists permanently

- Every one has to leave this world, even though he wishes not to. No magic can actually help a person to stay forever
- Everyone has their set life periods. One who is born, will die one day and will be born again according to his Karmas.

God is the cause of this creation

- Krishna is the incarnation of God, Parmatma or Ishvar by whatever name we call Him.
- God alone is the original cause of all causes.
- He starts everything and ends everything too.
- He is there everywhere. He is omnipresent and omnipotent
- We are just puppets whom he controls.

CHAPTER 16 - DIVINE AND THE DEMONIC QUALITIES

In Sixteenth chapter, Lord Krishna tells that in this world, there are two types of persons - those having divine qualities and those having demonic qualities. In first three verses, the qualities of divine persons have been briefly explained, which help one to gain Liberation and freedom from this World. In verses from 7 to 20, the qualities of persons with demonic qualities have been explained in details and such persons with demonic nature and qualities never gain Liberation but remain in this circle of birth and death. Lord Krishna further tells in this chapter that lust, anger and greed are the three gates to hell.

Virtues of saintly nature (Verse 1 – 3)

Shri Krishna describes in these three verses the twenty six virtues of those endowed with divine nature:

1. Fearlessness - Freedom from concern for present and future miseries, fear of death, and all types of losses in the life.
2. Purity of mind - Having good thoughts in the mind. Giving up deceit, cheating and falsehood in your interactions with people will naturally provide you purity of mind.

3. Pursuit for spiritual knowledge - Always remaining steadfast in spiritual principles.
4. Charity - to help the needy persons without any self motive.
5. Control of senses - Keeping the sense organs under control from sensual pleasures.
6. Performing Vedic rituals and other religious acts
7. Study of Vedic scriptures and contemplating on the same
8. Austerity - Religious discipline for purifying the body, mind and intellect.
9. Straightforwardness - Alignment in thought, word and deeds.
10. Ahinsa - Not to hurt any living being by any means – physical, oral or mental.
11. Truthfulness – Refraining oneself from distorting facts to suit one's purpose
12. Absence of anger – to overcome anger by developing detachment and surrender to the will of the God.
13. Renunciation - Giving up results of actions
14. Peacefulness - ability to retain inner equilibrium despite disturbing external situations.
15. Restraint from fault-finding - Not to talk or listen about shortcomings of others
16. Compassion towards all living beings – sympathy for those suffering or in pain.
17. Absence of greediness – freedom from desires and longing to accumulate wealth more than

what one legitimately needs for the maintenance of the body and family.
18. Gentleness – not to behave rudely with others
19. Modesty - Shying away from praise about oneself
20. Lack of fickleness (lack of nervousness) - not to get distracted by temptations and hardship and remain firm in pursuit to reach the goal.
21. Vigour - deep inner drive to act according to one's values and beliefs
22. Forgiveness or forbearance - ability to tolerate the offences of others, without feeling the need to retaliate.
23. Fortitude – inner strength and determination in pursuing the goal, even when the mind and senses are tired due to unfavourable circumstances.
24. Cleanliness - Inner and outer cleanliness
25. Enmity towards none - Not having enmity towards any one
26. Absence of Vanity or pride - Not demanding self respect from others

In the 4th verse, Bhagvaan briefly describes the six qualities of a person born with devil mind. These persons are **hypocrite** i.e. they proclaim themselves as followers of Dharma (righteousness) but in fact do actions not for the benefit of others but to cause them harm. They show **arrogance** and **pride** of their wealth and knowledge, demand respect from others which they do not deserve. They get **angry** on slightest pretext, **speak harshly** and they **lack in proper knowledge** to discriminate between right and wrong.

Divine qualities lead to Liberation while demonic qualities result into bondage. Lord Krishna tells Arjun not to grieve since you are born with divine qualities.

Shri Krishna then says that there are only two types of human beings in this world: The divine, or the wise; and the demonic, or the ignorant. The divine has been described at length; and now Lord Krishna describes in details about the qualities of demonic persons.

Qualities of persons of demonic nature; verses 7 - 18

Persons of demonic nature do not know what is right and wrong actions and thus they have neither purity nor good conduct nor truthfulness. They say, "The world is unreal, without any basis, without a God, and without an order, just born of union of man and woman alone driven by passion and nothing else." Thus, the demoniac-minded see engagement in lustful activities as the purpose of human life.

Adhering to these malicious and twisted views, these degraded souls with lower intellect and cruel deeds, do not hesitate to aggressively pursue their self-centered goals, even if it results in grief to others and destruction to the world. Resorting to desires that are difficult to be fulfilled, they become full of hypocrisy, pride and arrogance. Holding wrong views due to delusion, they disregard the injunctions of the scriptures and go contrary to what is proper and truthful.

They are obsessed with endless anxieties and desire that end only at death. They are convinced that gratification of desires and accumulation of wealth are the highest experience of joy. And enslaved by lust and anger, they strive to obtain wealth by unlawful means to fulfill sensual pleasures.

The demoniac persons deluded by ignorance think, "I have gained so much wealth today, and I shall now fulfill this desire of mine. I own this today, and tomorrow I shall have even more." In this way, their desires are unending and want to enjoy everything whatever gives them pleasure.

They boast, "That enemy has been destroyed by me, and I shall destroy the others too. I am like God myself, I am the enjoyer, I am all powerful and happy too."

They think, "I am rich and I have highly placed relatives. No one is equal to me, how can anyone be superior to me"? They even perform ritualistic ceremonies to accrue abundance and fame from celestial gods and rejoice in claiming to have given alms in charity.

Shri Krishna says, that such persons deluded by ignorance, bewildered by many fancies, entangled in the net of delusion, addicted to the enjoyment of sensual pleasures, they fall into unclean places like hell.

Such boastful, egocentric, filled with pride and intoxication of wealth, perform ritualistic ceremonies so as to look pious in the eyes of society but not according to scriptural injunction. These malicious people cling to egoism, power, arrogance, lust, and anger; and they deny presence of Parmatma in their own body and in others' bodies.

Repercussions of the demoniac mentality; verse 19 & 20

Shri Krishna says that those who are hateful, cruel, sinful, cunning, wicked and lowest level of mentality among mankind take birth into the wombs of those with similar demoniac natures in the cycle of birth and death in the material world. Such deluded souls take birth again and again in the wombs of demons according to their karmas. They thus gradually sink to the most abominable (lowest level) type of existence and never reach the Supreme Lord.

Last four shlokas of this chapter are again very important to understand properly. Bhagvaan again highlights that Lust, anger, and greed are the three gates of hell leading to the downfall of the individual. Therefore, one must learn to dread these three and carefully avoid their presence in their own personality.

Selfish desire or lust is the root of all evil. These devil qualities, such as anger, greed, attachment, pride, jealousy, hatred, and fraud, are born out of desire and are also called sin. Desire, when fulfilled, brings more desires, thereby breeding greed. Unfulfilled desires cause anger. Anger is a temporary insanity. People do sinful acts when they are angry. They who act in haste under the spell of anger repent afterwards. Ignorance of spiritual knowledge is responsible for lust; therefore, lust can be removed only by acquiring Self-knowledge. Lust also conceals Self-knowledge as a cloud covers the sun.

One must learn to control desires with contentment, and anger with forgiveness. They who have overcome desires have really conquered the world and live a peaceful, healthy, and happy life. One who is freed from these three gates of hell, endeavor for the welfare of their soul and consequently attain the supreme goal.

Lust, anger, and greed are the commanders of the army of illusion that must be defeated before Liberation is possible. One who acts under the influence of desires, disobeying the scriptures (not according to Dharma), neither attains perfection nor happiness, nor the Supreme Abode. Therefore, Shri Krishna says in last verse of this chapter, "let the scripture be your guide in determining what should be done and what should not be done. Perform your duties in this world in accordance with the teachings in the scriptures."

- HARI OM -
Thus ends the Sixteenth chapter entitled "DAIVASUR SAMPAD VIBHAG YOG"

Keep your ego under control - How?

Remember that...
- I am not the Owner of any thing, I am only a Possessor
- Every thing has been given to me and because it is given to me, it can be taken away any time.
- I am only a managing trustee of this body, mind and sense complex.
- Nothing is authored by me and therefore, I am not the owner
- Every thing in this world will temporary

Once you constantly remember this, your pride will go away and you will feel happiness within.

CHAPTER 17 – YOGA OF THREEFOLD SHRADHA

In last verse of Chapter 16, Bhagvaan had said that *'with reference to what is to be done and what not to be done, what is right and what is wrong, scriptures should be the means of knowing that'*. This creates a doubt in the mind of Arjun as to what happens if a person unknowingly, does not do what is enjoined in the scriptures. Therefore, Chapter 17 begins with this question of Arjun.

Arjun question is very relevant for each one of us, since sometimes, even though we know what is right; still we don't find people doing the right action. A thief knows that it is not proper to steal someone's property but still he steals since he knows what he is gaining but he does not know what he is losing if he steals. Only scriptures can provide complete knowledge of consequences of stealing.

A human being has been given the faculty of choice – the option to choose the right or wrong action, to steal or not to steal, to tell a lie or speak the truth, to hurt or refrain from hurting. At the same time, one must understand that the Law of Karmas go together with the faculty of choice given to human beings. A common sense has been given to all of us to know what is right and what is wrong. This universal sense of right or wrong is what is called

Dharma. It is known to every one without being taught about the natural laws – the law of gravity for example, even a baby monkey, clinging to its mothers stomach, knows that it will fall to the ground if it lets go off its mother while she is swinging from trees to trees. It is a universal law, not created by us and therefore true always and for everyone. A man-made law like laws of taxation, etc. may vary from country to country. These are different from the Dharmic fabric, the law of right and wrong, which is part of the creation. There is no way we can escape from these laws of the creation.

We have the freedom to perform action or avoid it, but we still do an action which we could have avoided and one will definitely get the result of his right or wrong action as per the Laws of Karma. You can always avoid the sight of a traffic police officer while jumping a red signal and not get caught, but you cannot avoid the detection or result of the action which is against the natural law. A robber knows what he gains by robbing some body and what money can do for him, but he does not know that the law of Karma produces an unseen result for every action. The scriptures tell us about this Law of Karma and also what should be done and what should not be done.

In Chapter 17, Lord Krishna says that every human being is born with innate faith (Shradha in Sanskrit) born out of three gunas - Sattvic, Rajasic, or Tamasic and does various actions, various rituals according to his Shradha.

Let us first understand what is Shradha?

Shradha is not an external object; it is within your mind, it is your thinking, your understanding, your value structure, your priorities. You may call it Faith or Belief, but it is much more than that, it is the whole person. It is your whole attitude towards life, attitude towards your body, mind, wealth, towards people, towards pooja, food, charity etc. The whole behavior of the person, his actions, the way he keeps his house, all indicate type of Shradha he has.

How can one perform rituals without expecting result?

In this chapter, it is said that all rituals like Yagya, Tap and charity which are Satvic are performed by a person without any result in view. The question arises, how one can perform karmas without expecting a result? Bhagvaan says that all these rituals and Dharmic karma are to be performed as an offering to Ishvar, in order to neutralize sins and thus for purifying your inner self and not for any physical gain. What all is meant here is that you should do all your Karmas which are enjoined by the Dharma, with a composed and cheerful mind for cleansing your inner self, and not getting swayed by other desires. Such rituals are called Satvic.

All this is explained in Chapter 17 by Lord Krishna from 2nd verse onwards.

In verse 1, Arjun asks Shri Krishna, "Please tell me what is the basis if a person performs an action or ritual not according to what is stipulated in the scriptures but according to his own faith or belief? Is that based on Satvic, Rajsic or Tamsic disposition?"

Bhagvaan first explains that every human being is born with innate faith (Shradha in Sanskrit) born out of three gunas - Sattvic, Rajasic, or Tamasic and then explains what Shradha is in verse 3? Shri Krishna states that the quality of one's faith of belief is based on the nature of his mind and decides the direction of his life. It describes the person as a whole, his natural character, his behaviour, his attitude towards life, his understanding and value structure etc. A person confirms exactly according to what Shradha he has.

Shradha from standpoint of worship; (Verse 4 – 6)

From standpoint of worship, Satvic people worship various gods or deities (like Indra, Varun, Agni, Vishnu, Shiva etc.), Rajsic people worship Yaksh and Rakshas and Tamsic people worship ghosts and other harmful spirits.

There are also some ignorant persons who perform severe religious practices, which are not according to the scriptures, just according to their own mind and for the purpose of showing their own power and pride. Their religious disciplines are driven by strong passions and longings and senselessly torture their own physical body and also disrespect the Soul that resides within. All these are contrary to the recommended path of the scriptures. Such people are known to be of devil nature.

Having explained the various categories of worship based on their innate faith, Shri Krishna now explains from verse 7 onwards, three categories of other disciplines in one's daily life activities.

Three types of food, we eat; (verse 8, 9 & 10)

- **Satvic** food – Persons of Satvic disposition prefer **Satvic** foods that promote longevity, virtue, strength, health, happiness, and joy, which are juicy, smooth, and nutritious.
- **Rajsic** food - foods that are very bitter, sour, salty, hot, pungent, dry, and burning, and cause pain, grief, and disease are Rajsic foods which are liked by people having **Rajsic** nature.
- **Tamsic** food - foods that are stale, tasteless, putrid, rotten, leftover, impure and unfit are liked by people having **Tamsic** nature.

Three types of worship or rituals; verse 11 - 13

- Satvic Rituals are those which are according to the scriptures and are performed without expecting any result in return except for purity of mind and intellect, and with firm conviction that these rituals

are to be done for benefit of mankind only. When rituals are performed in this manner, it is classified in the mode of goodness or Satvic.
- **Rajsic Rituals** - Rituals that are performed keeping in view the result and is done just for one's own glories are **Rajasic** in nature.
- **Tamsic** rituals – Rituals that are performed without having faith in God and without following the scripture, in which no food is offered, no mantras are chanted and no donation is made, are Tamsic in nature.

Religious discipline of body, mind and speech

Shri Krishna next describes in verses 14 – 16, the three ways of doing austerity (religious disciplines) called **tapah** in sanskrit – by deeds (by physical body), by words (by speaking) and by thought (by mind).

The worship of gods, the priest, the guru, and the wise; when done with observance of cleanliness, purity, honesty, celibacy, and nonviolence is said to be the austerity of the physical body.

Speech that is non-offensive, truthful, pleasant, beneficial, and is used for the regular recitation of scriptures is called the discipline of the speech.

Mental cheerfulness, gentleness, restraint in speaking, self-control, and the purity of thoughts are called the discipline of the Mind.

Three types of austerities; verses 17 - 19

The above mentioned threefold disciplines observed with supreme faith in a selfless manner, without attachment to rewards and without expecting any result are designated as Satvic tapah.

Austerity that is performed for gaining respect, honor, reverence, and for the sake of show off is said to be of the **Rajsic** nature. Its benefits are unstable and transitory.

Austerity performed by those who are having confused notions or ideas and which involve torturing oneself or harming others, is said to be of **Tamsic** nature. Such austerities accomplish nothing positive.

The three-fold divisions of dānam, or charity, are now being described in verses 20 to 22

Charity that is given to a deserving person at the right place and right time as a matter of his duty and without expecting anything in return, is considered to be **Satvic** charity.

Charity which is given for the sake of being helped in return or keeping in view of some benefit in future and which is given unwillingly causing a feeling of loss or pain is said to be **Rajsic** charity.

Charity which is given at a wrong place and time to unworthy persons, without showing respect or with a purpose to ridicule him, is said to be **Tamsic** charity.

Significance of three words - OM Tat Sat (verse 23 – 27)

In the next five shloka of this chapter, Shri Krishna introduces these three words "OM TAT SAT". Each of these three words independently and together reveals Brahman, the Absolute Reality. **Brahma ji** created everything in the beginning of creation – **Priests**, Vedas and Rituals, by saying these three words.

The syllable Om is a symbolic representation of the impersonal aspect of God. It is also considered as the name for the formless Brahman. It is also the primordial sound that pervades creation. Therefore, when performing any sacred act or rituals, OM is recited by the priest at the beginning of Vedic mantras to invoke auspiciousness. OM purifies everything, it is such a sacred sound that just by pronouncing it, your speech gets purified, your actions get purified.

TAT also means Param Braham – the cause of everything. The fruits of all actions belong to God, and hence, any yagya (sacrifice), tapaḥ (austerity), and dānam (charity), must be done by a person purely for purifying the mind and the inner self, with an attitude of offering to Bhagvaan. Chanting Tat along with austerity, sacrifice, and charity symbolizes that they are not performed for material rewards, but for the eternal welfare of the soul through God-realization. Generally Tat is not used alone but is used along with other two words in the expression "OM TAT SAT".

The word SAT has many connotations, and the two verses 26 & 27 describe some of these. SAT is used to mean perpetual goodness and virtue. In addition, auspicious performance of sacrifice, austerity, and charity is also described as SAT. SAT also means that which always exists i.e., it is an eternal truth, the only existence is **Parmeshvar**.

Thus these three words "OM TAT SAT" when used at the completion of any religious activity, all omissions and mistakes done unknowingly are made up for. But **OM** is used alone at the beginning of any undertaking of religious activity.

In the last verse of this chapter, Shri Krishna makes it clear that if you do any religious activity, or charity or pooja without Shradha in the existence of God, it has no meaning and it is as good as " not done". When a Havan is being done and ghee is offered to the fire by you thinking that I am wasting this ghee by offering to the fire, it could have been given to poor people, then that offering becomes useless. Or if you do some tapa like going to Haridwar during the month of Shravan, just for the sake of blindly following someone, or to show off or with a particular desire in mind, or as a picnic spot to enjoy company of other friends, having no Shradha at all, that tapah becomes useless, incapable of producing any merits in this life or next life either. They are as good as not done.

- HARI OM -
Thus ends the Seventeenth chapter entitled "SHRADHATRAY VIBHAG YOG"

CHAPTER 18 – MOKSH SANYAS YOG

In this Chapter 18, Lord Krishna has summed up the meaning of whole teachings given to Arjun in Shrimad Bhagavad-Gita so far. We have seen that there are two types of life styles mentioned for the pursuit of Liberation, Moksha - one is the life of total renunciation; Karm Sanyas and the other is the life of Karm Yog, the life of activity with a proper attitude, the attitude of a Karm Yogi or the attitude of Karm fal tyaga. A Sanyasi is absolved from all obligatory duties in order to pursue knowledge while a Karm Yogi retains the obligatory duties but doing these with proper attitude of giving up the attachments to the results of actions. A Sanyasi has no duties to perform while a Karm yogi has only duties to perform. Lord Krishna had explained all this in great details right from second chapter onwards.

We have also seen that Arjun had not understood which life style he should follow and therefore, he asked first in third chapter, "If you consider Renunciation is better than action, why do you ask me to indulge in this terrible action, you are confusing me by these contradictory statements, please tell me definitely one thing by which I will gain Liberation." Lord Krishna had explained the two life styles in details in third and fourth chapters and asked him to take up the life of a Karm Yogi. However, Arjun still was not convinced and again asked the same question at the beginning of the fifth chapter in different way: "you are praising both renunciation of actions and Karm Yog, please tell me definitely which is better for me?" Lord Krishna again explained that both of them are in fact one and same but Sanyas is difficult to accomplish without being a Yogi and moreover it is easier to be a Karm Yogi than being a Sanyasi. He also explains that real Sanyas is not mere renunciation of Karma but it is renunciation of all actions through knowledge.

After hearing the teachings in all these chapters, Arjun again asks the same question in beginning of Chapter 18, in different words asking what the difference between Sanyas and Tyag is. Lord Krishna obliges him by explaining the difference between Sanyas and Tyag in more details in chapter 18 in 40 verses. In subsequent verses, Lord Krishna describes four categories of people based on their Karm and how one can attain liberation while doing one's duties with devotion. After all these teachings and explanations, Arjun finally got ready to do his duties as a warrior and fight the Kaurvas in the battle field of Kurukshetra.

Difference between Sanyas and Tyag

Before we know the difference, first let us see what is meant by **Sanyas** and who is a **Sanyasi**?

Sanyas means complete renunciation of doer-ship, ownership, and personal selfish motive behind an action. A **Sanyasi** is one who does not own anything. A true **Sanyasi** works for others and lives for others. **Sanyas** does not mean living in the forest or any other secluded place outside society. **Sanyas** is a state of mind that is completely detached from the outcome or the fruits of actions.

Whereas **Tyag** means renunciation of the selfish attachment to the fruits of all actions, and doing work which are to be done considering as one's duty and dedicated to God. A person who does actions enjoined by one's Dharma with the attitude of selfless services for the sake of mankind and purification of his mind and intellect, is called a **Tyagi** or a **Karm Yogi**.

The words **"Sanyas"** and **"Tyag"** are used interchangeably throughout the Gita because there is no real difference between the two. Renunciation of attachment to sensual pleasures is the real sacrifice or real **Tyaga**. The perfection of **Tyag** comes only after a person becomes free from the clutches of attachments and aversions, likes and dislikes. Bhagvaan Krishna says **Karm Yog** has to be done while living in this world and not by renunciation of the world, as is commonly misinterpreted. Selfless service or **Tyag** is the essence of the teachings as given in this last chapter. A person who is **Tyagi** cannot commit sin and is released from the cycles of birth and death. One can cross the ocean of transmigration and reach the shores of liberation in this very life by the boat of **Tyag**.

Everybody desires peace of mind, but that is only possible if one does his duties without being attached to its results and dedicates the results of all actions to God. This is not necessarily the same as offering all his material wealth and possessions to someone or to his children or his Guru or give in charity to some trust etc. Doing one's duty, earning wealth, material enjoyment, and attaining liberation are the four noble goals of human life for the householder in the Vedic tradition. One, who is engaged only in earning wealth and sense gratification, abandoning one's duty, soon gets into trouble. But one who does his duty righteously and then earns wealth and enjoys sensual pleasure in a balanced manner without harming any one, attains liberation. One should first follow Dharma by doing one's duty righteously. Then one should earn money and make economic progress, fulfill all noble material and spiritual desires with the money earned, and progress towards liberation, the only noble goal of human birth. The wise person considers contentment as the supreme pleasure and remembers that he is just the trustee of all wealth and possessions whatever have been given to him since everyone comes in this world with empty hands and goes empty handed.

There are Nine Types of Renunciation mentioned in Gita, which can help gain liberation:

1. Renunciation of actions forbidden by the scriptures,
2. Renunciation of lust, anger, greed, fear, likes and dislikes, and jealousy ;
3. Giving up results of actions in the search of Truth
4. Giving up the feeling of pride in one's knowledge, detachment, devotion, wealth, and charitable deeds;

5. Rejection of selfish motives and attachment to the fruits of all actions
6. Renunciation of the feeling of doer-ship in all undertakings
7. Giving up thoughts of using the Lord to fulfill selfish, material desires
8. Giving up attachments to material objects, such as a house, wealth, position, and power; and
9. Sacrifice of wealth, prestige, and even life for a noble cause and protection of righteousness (Dharma).

In first verse itself, Arjun asks Shri Krishna; please tell me distinctly the difference that exists between "**sanyās**" and "**tyāg**". Shri Krishna understanding the spirit of the question gives an elaborate and all inclusive answer.

Difference between sanyās and tyāg

Shri Krishna says, "Learned people consider sanyās as giving up of all actions motivated by desires. While the wise men declare that giving up attachment to the fruits of actions is tyāg." Sanyāsīs continue to do some of the nitya Karm (daily works) for the maintenance of the body, but they renounce kāmya Karm, the Vedic rituals related to acquisition of wealth, progeny, prestige, status, power, etc. While on the other hand, the tyagis do not relinquish the kāmya Karm, rather they renounce the desires for enjoying their fruits.

Then there are some philosophers who say that all actions are inherently defective and hence should be given up while others say that religious rituals, charity and austerity should not be given up. Shri Krishna tells Arjun that now I will give you the final verdict on the renunciation. He says that he will expound upon the subject by dividing renunciation into three categories.

Real meaning of renunciation – tyag; verses 5 - 12

The acts of service, charity, and austerity should not be given up, but indeed should be performed because these acts of services, charity and religious disciplines bring about self purification for the wise person. Shri Krishna says, "My supreme advice is that even these obligatory actions should be done with the attitude of giving up the attachment to the fruits of these actions. Therefore, renunciation of one's duty is not proper."

Shri Krishna states that prescribed duties should never be renounced. Giving up prescribed duties in the name of renunciation is said to be of Tamsic nature. Having come in this world, we all have obligatory duties. For an ordinary person, acts such as earning wealth, taking care of the family, bathing, eating, etc. are prescribed duties. One should always perform his obligatory duties and abandoning them, out of ignorance, leads to the degradation of the soul.

To give up prescribed duties because they are troublesome or cause bodily discomfort is Rajsic renunciation. Such renunciation is never beneficial and do not elevate their soul on spiritual level.

When one continues to perform his obligatory duties, but gives up attachment to the fruit of actions, this is the highest kind of renunciation, which is of Sattvic mode.

Those who avoid works that cause them do not discomfort nor do they get attached to those works which are agreeable to them, are true renunciant. They are endowed with the quality of the Sattvic mode. They simply do their duty under all conditions, without feeling elated when the going is good or feeling dejected when life becomes tough.

Human beings cannot completely abandon actions; therefore, one who completely renounces selfish attachment to the fruits of all actions is considered a true tyagi.

The three-fold fruits of actions - desirable, undesirable and mixed, accrue even after death to those who are attached to the personal reward of their results. But for those who renounce the fruits of their actions, there are no such results in this life or next life.

What constitutes Action? – verse 13 - 14

Shri Krishna announces to Arjun that he is now going to tell him five constituents of actions as described in

Sankhy philosophy, as this knowledge will help develop detachment from the results of actions. These are:

- The physical body, which is the basis for performing all actions
- The doer – refers here to the soul situated in the body which inspires the body-mind-intellect mechanism with the life force to act.
- The instruments with which the actions are performed, these are organs of action and senses, the mind and the intellect. It is with their help that the doer, the soul accomplishes various kinds of work.
- The cheṣhṭā (effort) is another ingredient of action. Despite all the instruments of action, if one does not put in effort, nothing is ever done. And for putting efforts, you require energy and that is supplied by Prana. Prana consists of various separate functions of respiration, evacuation, circulation, digestion and the reversal of physiological functions.
- The fifth factor is the Divine Providence or the laws according to which all these organs of the body function. This is called destiny also which is based on the results of our auspicious and inauspicious deeds in previous life. It is God also seated within the body of living beings as witness, who bestows people with abilities, in accordance with their past karmas. He also grants the results of the present karmas.

Karmic reactions of actions; verses 15 - 17

The above five are the causes of all actions, whether right or wrong, which a man performs by thought, word, and deeds. Therefore, the person who considers his own self as the doer of all actions does not see correctly due to imperfect knowledge. He does not see that Atma is independent of this body and Atma is not the doer. If the soul were not granted a body by God, it could not have done anything at all. Further, if the soul was not energized by God, it could have still not done anything.

Therefore, those who are free from false pride of being the doer and who do not seek to enjoy the fruits of actions, they are not bound in the karmic reactions of what they do. From material perspective, they may kill some living beings, but from spiritual perspective, they are free from selfish motivation and therefore are not bound by the results of karmas.

Constituents of action – verse 18 & 19

Shri Krishna then explains that there are threefold driving force for an action. These are **gyān** (knowledge), gyeya (the object of knowledge), and gyātā (the knower), these three together are called 'triad of knowledge'. Knowledge is a primary impetus for action; since it provides understanding and prescribed means to the knower about what is to be known. Then, there are three constituents of action called 'triad of action'. It includes the **kartā** (doer), **kāraṇ** (the instrument of doing action which are eleven organs consisting of organs of action, sense organs and the mind), and **Karm** (the act itself). The doer utilizes the instruments of action to perform the action.

Therefore, **gyān** (Knowledge), **Karm** (action) and **kartā**, the doer are the three main constituents of action. Having analyzed the constituents of action, Shri Krishna now relates them to the three modes of gunas, to explain why people differ from each other in their motives and actions as enumerated in the scriptures. Lord Krishna thus explains each of these three now.

Three modes of Knowledge (verse 20 – 22)

Sāttvic knowledge is one by which a person sees one undivided imperishable reality within all diverse living beings. Creation gives the appearance of a panorama of diverse living beings and material entities. But the substratum behind this apparent diversity is the Supreme Lord. A person having Sattvic knowledge see the unity that exists behind the variety of creation, just as an electrical engineer sees the same electricity flowing through different gadgets, and a goldsmith sees the same gold cast into different ornaments.

He knows that God is one without a second; He is one with all similar entities since these are different manifestations of the one God. All other souls are his tiny fragmental parts. A fragment is one with its whole, just as flames are one with the fire of which they are tiny parts.

Maya which is dissimilar to God is insentient, while God is sentient. However, Maya is energy of God, and energy is one with its energetic, just as the energies of fire, heat and light are non-different from each other. Maya and the soul are both dependent upon God for their existence. If God did not energize them, they would cease to exist. On the other hand, God is supremely independent and does not need the support of any other entity for His existence.

On the other hand, **Rajasic knowledge** is that by which one sees the manifold living beings in diverse bodies as individuals and does not perceive them as connected to one God. Rajasic knowledge thus divides the human beings with distinctions of race, class, creed, sect, nationality, etc.

Whereas, that knowledge by which one remains engrossed to his body alone as if it were everything and the complete truth. Their understanding is usually neither rational, nor grounded in the scriptures or in reality, and yet they try to impose their beliefs on others. Such irrational knowledge is **Tamsic** knowledge.

Three modes of Action (verse 23 – 25)

The actions which are to be done as obligatory duty and are performed without being impelled by likes and dislikes and done without selfish motives and attachment to the results is called Satvic Karm.

But the Action performed with arrogance and lot of efforts, with selfish motives is called the Rajsic Karm.

That action which is undertaken because of delusion, disregarding natural consequences, loss, injury to others, as well as one's own ability, is Tamsic in nature.

Three modes of karta (doer) (verse 26 – 28)

Sāttvic doers are 'mukta sangaḥ', i.e. they do not work for the sake of worldly pleasures, nor do they believe that worldly things can bestow satisfaction upon the soul. Hence, they work with noble motives. And since their intentions are pure, they are filled with zeal and strong resolve in their endeavors. They are free from egotism and give all credit for their success to God. They do not get perturbed in success and failure.

Rajasic doers are deeply ambitious for materialistic enhancement and therefore have never ending desires. They are never satisfied by what comes their way and are always greedy for more and more. They do not possess the purity of intention and in order to fulfill their desires, they sacrifice morality and even become violent. When their desires are fulfilled they become elated, and when they are not met they get dejected. In this way, their lives become a mixture of joys and sorrows.

Tamasic doers are undisciplined i.e. they do not follow the injunctions given in scriptures regarding what is proper and improper behavior. They are obstinate in their views and have closed ears and mind to others views. Thus, they are often cunning, vulgar and dishonest in their ways. Though they may have duties to perform, they see effort as laborious and painful, and so they are lazy and try to postpone the work. Their infamous thoughts impact them more than anyone else, making them unhappy and sad.

After having explained the constituents of action, Shri Krishna now explains in **verse 29** that there are two factors that impact the quality and quantity of work. They not only propel action but also control and direct it. These are the **Buddhi** (intellect) and **Dhriti** (determination). Buddhi is the faculty of discrimination that distinguishes between right and wrong. Dhriti is the inner determination to persist in accomplishing the work undertaken, despite hardships and obstacles on the way. Both are of three kinds in accordance with the gunas.

Three kinds of Intellect (verse 30 – 32)

The Sattvic mode of goodness illumines the intellect with the light of knowledge thereby refining its ability to discriminate what is right action and what is wrong action. The Sattvic intellect is one that makes known to us what type of action is to be performed and what type of action is to be renounced, what is to be feared and what is not to be feared. It truly understands what bondage is and what liberation is.

The intellect which is confused and cannot distinguish between righteousness and unrighteousness is Rajasic intellect. The person of Rajasic intellect is unable to discern the proper course of action due to their attachments and aversions, likes and dislikes. He is confused between the important and the trivial, the permanent and the transient, the valuable and the insignificant.

The Tamasic intellect is one that is shrouded in ignorance without the illumination of sublime knowledge. Hence, it misconstrues adharma as dharma, right as wrong and so on. In the Tamasic intellect, the faculty of judgment and the ability for logical reasoning become lost.

Three kinds of Determination (Dhriti); verse 33 - 35

The steadfast willpower that is developed through the practice of Yog, so that one learns to subdue the senses, discipline the life-airs (prana), and control the mind is Sattvic dhṛiti (determination in the mode of goodness).

The determination, by which one holds on to duty out of attachment to pleasures and wealth and desire for enjoying the rewards, is Rajasic dhṛiti.

The determination by which a person having improper thinking, does not give up sleep, fear, grief, despair, and carelessness, is Tamsic dhṛiti. Such determination based upon stubborn clinging to unproductive thoughts is of the mode of ignorance.

In the previous verses, Shri Krishna discussed the constituents of action and the factors that motivate and control action. Shri Krishna now goes on to explain the goal of action. The ultimate motive behind human actions is the search for happiness. Everyone desires to be happy, and through their actions they seek fulfillment, peace, and satisfaction. Shri Krishna says that happiness is also of three categories and explains each of these in verse 37- 39.

The happiness or joy that one discovers from spiritual practice for purifying the mind, which may appear as poison in the beginning, but is like nectar in the end, that happiness is called Satvic Happiness born of the clarity of Self-knowledge.

Happiness when it is derived from the contact between the senses and their objects, which appears as nectar in the beginning, but changes like a poison in the end is Rajsic Happiness. Such joy is short-lived and leaves in its wake greed, anxiety and guilt and thus keeps the person in the realm of material world which is full of miseries. The path to lasting and divine bliss lies not in indulgence, but in renunciation, austerities, and discipline.

The happiness or pleasures derived from sleep, laziness, and negligence is called Tamsic happiness. The Tamsic happiness covers the person's intellect with ignorance about the true nature of the Self both in the beginning and in the end. Worldly pleasures are like a mirage in the desert. Thirsty persons reckon it as water until they come to drink it and find nothing.

Summing up, Lord Krishna says in verse 40 that there is no human being, either on the earth or among the gods in the heaven, who can remain free from the influence of these three gunas born of Material Nature or Maya of Bhagvaan. The three modes of nature—sattva, rajas, and Tamas—are inherent attributes of Maya; they exist in all the material abodes of existence.

Now, using these three modes of Prakriti, Shri Krishna explains why human beings possess different natures, according to the guṇas that constitute their personality. Shri Krishna explains that people have different natures, according to the guṇas that constitute their personality, and thus different professional duties are suitable for them. The system of varṇāshram was a scientific organization of society according to one's inherent nature and guṇas and not according to birth; **(Verses 41 – 44).**

In this system of categorization, four varṇas based on their duties in the society have been defined. These four categories are - Brahmin, Kshtriya, Vaishy and Shudr. The varṇas were not considered higher or lower amongst themselves. Since the center of society was God, everyone worked according to their intrinsic qualities to sustain themselves and society. Thus, in this system, there was unity in diversity like various limbs of our body perform different functions. Similarly, various human beings in the society perform different work matching with their nature and capabilities. The duties of each of these four categories of people described by Lord Krishna are as follows:

Brahmins - Those who possessed mostly *Sattvic* natures were the Brahmins. Their primary duties were to undertake austerities, practice purity of mind, do rituals according to scriptures. Thus, they were expected to be tolerant, humble, and spiritually minded. Profession of teaching, sharing their knowledge with others was most suitable for them.

Kshtriya - Those whose natures were predominantly Rajasic along with sattva guna were known as Kshtriya. Valor, strength, fortitude, large heartedness in charity, skill in weaponry and leadership are their main abilities. They never run away from the battle field and therefore, their main duty was to protect the society and the country they live in.

Vaishy - Those whose natures were predominantly Rajasic with a mixture of tamo guna were called Vaishy. They were thus inclined toward producing and possessing economic wealth through business and agriculture. They sustained the economy of the nation and created jobs for the other classes. They were also expected to undertake charitable projects to share their wealth with the deprived sections of society.

Shudr - Those who possessed mainly Tamasic natures were known as Shudr. Therefore to serve the society according to their specific ability is the natural duty of these persons, generally known as labor class.

These four designations or types are not determined by birth but based on the duties or work they do in the society born out of their own nature. A man gains success who delights in doing his own natural duties.

Doing one's own duties is far superior; (verses 46 – 48)

Lord Krishna now tells how one attains perfection while engaged in one's own duties.

By performing one's natural duties, one worships the Creator from whom all living entities have come into being, and by whom the whole universe is pervaded. By such performance of work, a person easily attains perfection.

One's own duty, even if it may be inferior, is better than the duty of another, even though well performed. One who does his duties ordained by one's inherent nature, without any selfish motive, does not incur sin.

One should not abandon the work that is best suited to his nature, even if it has defects in it, rather he should keep working according to his natural tendency. Shri Krishna states that no work is free from defect, just as fire naturally has smoke on top of it.

Lord Krishna again repeats in verse 49 that a Karm yogi who performs his duties keeping the mind and intellect unaffected by the stream of events, putting his best efforts without any selfish attachment to the fruits of work but as an act of worshiping the God, attains highest perfection of freedom from bondage of Karm.

How a Karm Yogi attains Supreme Bliss – verse 50 - 53

Shri Krishna has been explaining so far how we can attain perfection in spiritual practice by performing our duties with the attitude of Karm Yog. The consistent performance of Karm Yog results in the realization of spiritual knowledge and when one attains the perfection of Nishkam Karm Yog, the spiritual knowledge and God-realization becomes available through experience.

Shri Krishna explains how this happens in the next few verses. He now describes the excellence that is required for the perfection of Brahman-realization through practice of Karm Yog. That person becomes fit for attaining oneness with the Supreme Lord, when:

- One develops a purified intellect that is established in spiritual knowledge,
- The mind is firmly controlled from sensual pleasures by not indulging in likes and dislikes.
- The impulses of the body and speech are tenaciously disciplined.

- The activities for bodily maintenance, such as eating and sleeping, are wisely held in balance.
- He is deeply contemplative, and hence prefers to live in a quiet place and thus ever engaged in meditation
- The ego and its lust for power and prestige are dissolved
- The mind is tranquil and free from the bonds of desire, anger, greed and physical possessions.

Shri Krishna says, such a yogi attains realization of the Absolute Truth as Brahman.

The state of God realization; Verse 54 - 56

Shri Krishna now concludes the description of the stage of perfection.

The yogi thus situated in the state of Brahman realization is prasannātmā, meaning serene and unaffected by turbid and painful experiences. He neither grieves nor desires for anything. He does not crave for any material thing because he has realized that he is already complete and whole. Such a yogi sees all living beings with equal vision, realizing the substratum of Brahman in all of them. He thus attains the highest divine love (Bhakti) for God.

Shri Krishna says that it is only through pure devotion, one can come to know the true essence of God's personality and having known the true essence of God, one immediately merges with the Supreme Lord. It is through Bhakti that one enters into this secret and achieves full God-consciousness.

A devotee sees God in everything and everywhere. He sees his body, mind, and intellect as the energies of God; he sees all his material possessions as the property of God; he sees all living beings as parts and parcels of God. A devotee performs all kinds of his duties renouncing the pride of being the doer and enjoyer of work. He rather sees all work as devotional service to the God dedicating its result upon Him. Then, upon leaving the body, they go to the divine abode of God by His grace.

Union of Intellect with God – Buddhi Yog (verse 57)

Shri Krishna then asks Arjun to practice 'Buddhi Yog' meaning to unite the intellect with God. This union of the intellect with God occurs when it is firmly convinced that everything in existence has emanated from God, is connected to God, and all works are meant for His pleasures. Therefore, Shri Krishna asks Arjun to cultivate the intellect with proper knowledge and use it to guide the mind in the proper direction; only then the chitta will easily get attached to God. Only human beings have been given the intellect by God and intellect alone possesses the ability to control the mind.

The intellect is one of the four aspects of subtle 'antaḥkaraṇ' present in our body, which we commonly call as heart. When it creates thoughts, we call it mana, or mind. When it analyses and decides, we call it Buddhi, or intellect. When it gets attached to an object or person, we call it chitta. When it identifies with the attributes of the body and becomes proud, we call it ahankār, or ego. In this internal subtle body, the position of the intellect is dominant. It makes decision, while the mind thinks in accordance with those decisions, and the chitta gets attached to the objects of affection.

After advising Arjun to unite his intellect in God alone, Shri Krishna tells in **verse 58 to 60** the benefits of following his advice and the repercussions of not following it.

If we take full shelter of the Lord, with the mind fixed upon Him, then by His grace all obstacles and difficulties will be resolved. But if, out of pride, we disregard the instructions, thinking we know better than the eternal wisdom of God and the scriptures, we will fail to attain the goal of human life.

We should not think we have complete liberty to do what we wish. The soul does not lead an independent existence; it is dependent upon God's creation in many ways. In the materially bound state, it is under the influence of the three guṇas. The combination of guṇas creates our nature, and according to its dictates, we are compelled to act. Hence, we do not have absolute freedom to say, "I will do what I like." Shri Krishna thus warns Arjun that by nature he is a warrior, and if, out of pride, he decides not to fight, his Kshatriya nature will still compel him to fight.

Shri Krishna further elaborates to Arjun that "even if you wish not to fight out of delusion, your inborn qualities of heroism, chivalry, and patriotism will compel you to fight. Your nature and inclinations are such that you vehemently oppose evil wherever you see it. Therefore, it is beneficial for you to fight in accordance with my instructions, rather than be compelled by your nature to do the same."

Eternal bliss can be attained only by loving devotion to Bhagvaan; (Verses 61 & 62)

Thus all human beings are controlled by their own nature-born Karmic impressions. Therefore, we will be forced to do what we do not wish to do out of delusion. The Supreme Lord as *'Ishvar'* abiding in the heart of all beings causes them to move and revolve by the magic of His Maya (illusion) like a puppet of Karm created by the free-will mounted on a machine. *'Ishvar'* alone organizes, controls, and directs everything in the universe according to the Karmic laws.

In other words, we always remain under God dominion. The body in which one resides is a machine made from His material energy. Based upon one's past karmas, God have given the kind of body one deserved and God dwelling in the hearts of all living beings keeps note of all thoughts, words, and deeds of every soul. He judges all karmas whatever we do in the present life and based on that He alone decides our future. No one is independent of God in any condition. Hence Shri Krishna advises Arjun, to surrender to Him with loving devotion and follow His advice which is in your own best self-interest.

Shri Krishna emphasizes in verse 62 that one can attain absolute peace and eternal abode only by grace of God. However, to receive that grace, the *'Jeevatma'* (individual soul) must qualify itself by surrendering to God with loving devotion whole heartedly. Even a worldly father will not hand over all his precious possessions to his child until the child becomes responsible enough to utilize them properly. Similarly, the grace of God is not a whimsical act; He has perfectly rational rules on the basis of which He bestows it.

In Śhrīmad Bhāgavatam it is stated that "Giving up all forms of mundane social and religious conventions, simply surrender unto the Supreme Soul of all souls. Only then one can cross over this material ocean and become fearless."

In Ramayan also, it is said that "moment the soul surrenders to God, its account of sinful deeds in endless past lifetimes is destroyed by His grace."

How we should surrender to God? Six aspects have been described in the shruti:

1. **To desire only in accordance with the desire of God**, meaning that we must learn to be happy in the happiness of God.

2. **Not to desire against the desire of God**, meaning that not to complain about whatever God gives us.

3. **To have firm faith that God is protecting us.**

4. **To maintain an attitude of gratitude toward God**. We have received so many priceless gifts from the Lord. The earth that we walk upon, the sunlight which gives us energy, the air that we breathe, and the water that we drink, are all given to us by God. We should have an attitude of gratitude towards God for all this.

5. **To see everything we possess as belonging to God**. Remember that God created this entire world; hence, the true owner of everything is God alone. This world and everything in it belongs to God.

6. **To keep an attitude of humbleness**, if I was able to do something nice, it was only because God inspired my intellect in the right direction. Left to myself, I would never have been able to do it.

CONCLUSION OF GITA TEACHINGS

Having explained all the knowledge, Lord Krishna still noticed Arjun not getting up to fight. Therefore in verse 63, Shri Krishna tells Arjun that "I have revealed to you the most profound and confidential knowledge. Now the choice is in your hands."

The free will and the freedom of choice have been given by God to all human beings. The freedom of choice is not infinite. One cannot decide, "I choose to be the most intelligent person in the world." Our choices are limited by our past and present karmas. However, we do possess a certain amount of free will; we may or may not choose to surrender to God and exercise our love to Him. This decision has to be made by the soul itself; even all powerful God cannot force us to love Him. Therefore, Shri Krishna is calling Arjun's attention to his free will and asking him to choose to fight or not to fight.

And then tells Arjun that since you are most dear to me, I will once again reveal to you the most confidential of all knowledge. Thus in next two verses 65 & 66, Shri Krishna finally concludes the whole Gita teaching:

Lord Krishna tells Arjun that since you are my very dear friend, I pledge to you that you will certainly reach me. You simply have to – "always think of me, be my devotee, worship me fixing your mind upon me, offer service to me and bow down to me". Shri Krishna thus asks Arjun to engage in devotion of the Supreme Lord wholeheartedly. This is also the essence of all scriptures. And again asks Arjun again in next verse "to abandon attachment to results of all his duties and just surrender completely to my will with firm faith and loving devotion. I shall liberate you from all sins, the bonds of Karma; do not fear."

Bhagvaan says that in order to be free from pious or impious results that bind one to this material world, it is necessary to offer every action to God. When one voluntarily depends on the supreme Lord under all circumstances, then the good (Puny) and bad results (sins) of work automatically go to Him, and one is free from sin. Surrendering to God does not involve leaving the world, but realizing that everything happens in accordance with His laws and by His direction and power. Surrender to God is the complete renunciation of individual existence or the ego.

IMPORTANCE OF GITA TEACHINGS (verse 67 – 71)

In verse 67, Shri Krishna instructs Arjun not to divulge this knowledge to those who do not have faith in God and who are not His devotee. It should not be given to those who are averse to listening to spiritual topics and particularly to those who are envious of Bhagvaan existence.

However this most secret knowledge should be given to those who are devotees of God and perform devotional service to Bhagvaan. Shri Krishna says that those who teach this knowledge to my devotees shall certainly come to me, without any doubt. Shri Krishna further states that sharing this knowledge is the highest loving service one can render to God and they are the ones who are most dear to God on this earth. Hence, those who study and recite this sacred dialogue between Lord Krishna and Arjun are in fact performing the most holy act of propagation and acquisition of Self-Knowledge with their intellect. Even those who listen to this knowledge with faith and without envy, will gradually become purified; will be liberated from sins and attain the auspicious abodes of those who do Puny karmas.

Finally Arjuna gets ready to fight (verse 72 – 73)

Having told the importance of Gita teachings in above five verses, Lord Krishna asks Arjun, "Have you listened to this with single-minded attention? Has your delusion born of ignorance been completely destroyed?

Now Arjuna finally answers: "By Your grace my delusion is destroyed; I have gained Self-knowledge; my confusion with regard to body and soul is dispelled; and I shall obey your command."

In last five verses 74 – 78, Sanjay comes to the end of his narration of the divine discourse of the Bhagavad Gita. Sanjay says this wonderful dialogue between Lord Krishna and Arjun was heard and seen by him directly from Shri Krishna, the Lord of Yog himself due to the divine eyes granted to him by sage Vyas. And Sanjay further narrated the same to King Dhritrashtra telling him that he is greatly amazed and he is rejoicing it over and over again.

Sanjay tells Dhritrashtra "it is my conviction that wherever there is Krishna, the Lord of yoga and Arjun with the weapons of duty and protection, there will be everlasting prosperity, victory, happiness, and morality".

- HARI OM –

Thus ends the Eighteenth chapter entitled "MOKSH SANYAS YOG"

THE COMPLETE TEACHING OF GITA IN BRIEF

your real identity is not this physical body but the Atma in the form of pure awareness which lives in every physical body and this Atma is equated to Paramatma.

Parmeshvar is pure awareness and therefore not subject to time, space or attributes. It is pure satya (Absolute Truth), pure existence and limitless, which is the basis of everything in the universe.

There is nothing that is independent of this satya, that is Param Brahm or Paramatma.

CPSIA information can be obtained
at www.ICGtesting.com
Printed in the USA
LVHW020753010621
689025LV00004B/121

9 781636 402161